for Margo, Roni, Avigail and Cherna

Acknowledgments

My thanks are due to many people. First, to Jacqueline Kronberg, who taught me theatre games and introduced me to the world of creativity exercises. Second, to Ted Kazanoff, who taught me acting. Next, the late Professor Shimon Sachs, of Tel-Aviv University and the Israel Ministry of Education, who gave me the opportunity of teaching creativity games and exercises to remedial teachers, and who originally encouraged me to write this book.

I must also thank my wife Margo, for her help in preparing the manuscript, and her understanding when I was too busy to do my fair share of the household chores.

Lastly, my heartfelt thanks are due to all those children, teenagers, and adults, who attended my workshops and gave me so much invaluable feedback, and without whose enthusiasm and inventiveness, I would not have enjoyed so many wonderful hours of creative adventure.

Theatre Games
and Beyond

A creative approach for performers

Amiel Schotz

MERIWETHER PUBLISHING LTD.
Colorado Springs, Colorado

Meriwether Publishing Ltd., Publisher
P.O. Box 7710
Colorado Springs, CO 80933

Editor: Theodore O. Zapel
Typesetting: Sharon E. Garlock
Cover design: Janice Melvin
Interior illustrations: Janice Melvin, Amiel Schotz, workshop participants

© Copyright MCMXCVIII Meriwether Publishing Ltd.
Printed in the United States of America
First Edition

"Nursery Chairs: The Third Chair". from WHEN WE WERE VERY YOUNG by A.A. Milne Illustrations by E. H. Shepard. Copyright 1924 by E. P. Dutton, renewed 1952 by A. A. Milne. Used by permision of Dutton Children's Books, a division of Penguin Books USA Inc.

Library of Congress Cataloging-in-Publication Data

Schotz, Amiel, 1936-
        Theatre games and beyond : a creative approach for performers
    / Amiel Schotz. -- 1st ed.
        p.   cm.
    Includes bibliographical references.
    ISBN 1-56608-039-8 (paper)
    1. Improvisation (Acting)   2. Acting.   3. Games.   I. Title.
PN2071.15S36   1998
792'.028--dc21
                                                                98-9460
                                                      ⟶   CIP

1   2   3   4   5   6   7   8   9   99   98

CONTENTS

PREFACE

For Whom This Book Is Written

I have been passionately interested in theatre all my life and have been fortunate enough to have been instructed by some very fine teachers. They include Jacqueline Kronberg, a former member of Chicago's *Second City Theater*, who introduced me to theatre games, and Ted Kazanoff, under whom I studied acting at Brandeis University. Later, when I was teaching acting in the theatre department of Tel-Aviv University, I was asked to conduct Theatre and Creativity Games classes and workshops in that university's department of education.

This experience plunged me into an exhilarating new world, and I came to realize just how valuable theatre training techniques can be throughout the entire educational field. Since then, I have enthusiastically pursued this line of investigation in the most practical of all possible ways. I have worked with teachers and students, preschoolers, at risk and exceptional children, groups of foster parents, army officers in charge of cultural and educational activities, adults in evening classes, pensioners, and kids at summer camp. I hope I have helped some of these people to widen their horizons and learn something about themselves. I know that their creativity, curiosity, spontaneity and constant feedback have taught me more than I ever dreamed of when I started.

I do not claim to be the originator of more than a few of the games described here. Many of them are derived from acting and mime exercises and theatre games, some stem from traditional children's games, while others have been suggested by teachers and other participants in my workshops. In most cases, however, they are applied in a wider context than before and I suggest ways in which variations of the games can be devised for specific groups.

So this book has been written for myself, for all those who work with groups of people from kindergarten to the aged, and for all those who like, or would like, to play.

How the Book Is Organized

For the sake of convenience I have grouped the games and exercises under general headings such as *Group Orientation, Trust,*

Developing the Senses, and so on. I should make it clear that there is tremendous overlap and that virtually all of the games involve several elements simultaneously. Thus "reality" games may require considerable coordination and cooperation with other players and will also help to develop the senses. Some qualities, such as concentration or relaxation, are so integral to all the games that I have not listed them as a separate category.

The book starts with a general introduction, but a great deal of further explanatory material is incorporated in the descriptions of the games themselves. Readers will find that many of the comments and examples appearing under one heading are not irrelevant to other sections.

Exercises

A major theme running through this book is that individual players, group leaders and teachers can and should devise variations of the games, or add to the repertoire by adapting others they know about, or creating new ones. In addition, suggestions for further exercises are offered after many of the games and most sections.

Sample Workshops

In the Appendix, a number of sample workshop formats are offered that are suited to various age groups. However, these are only rough guides, and actual workshop sessions rarely conform exactly to plan. Often, one game is so successful that it takes up much more time than originally planned, or an incident in the session sparks off a diversion. These deviations from the plan are to be welcomed, and flexibility is no bad thing, as long as there is *some* structure to the session.

Apology

I have made some attempt to avoid referring to people of both sexes as "him," but I confess that sometimes I have found the needed grammatical circumlocutions just too clumsy and have then fallen back on the masculine pronoun to represent both male and female. No discrimination is intended.

INTRODUCTION

Avoid compulsion, and let your children's lessons take the form of play.

Plato, *The Republic*

Creativity and Play

Two puppies are playing in the garden outside my window. They leap at each other, roll over, snarl and make mock bites. Now one is on top, now the other. They break off to run across the grass, sniff at a tree and then resume their game. They are joined by a larger dog who fights and conquers each in turn. Suddenly they combine against him and he rolls over on his back. Tails wag, tongues loll, a scene of perfect contentment and energy.

Play is an essential activity. As babies and children we explore our environment, discover ourselves, develop our capabilities and our imagination, test our strengths and form relationships with one another, all through the medium of play. For the child, play "is often the totality of experience, it is his task, his work and his natural means of expression" (Marzollo and Lloyd, *Learning Through Play*).

Although psychologists differ in their analyses of the nature and functions of play, there is some consensus on the various stages of play which emerge as children naturally develop. However, it should be remembered that these stages overlap, continuing in parallel and in interaction with each other throughout our lives.

The first stage is *functional play*, when we begin to discover our own bodies and learn to control simple muscular activity. Touching, stretching and crawling, examining toys and objects, children begin to learn about the world around them. We also discover our own voices and reach toward vocal communication, cooing, chattering, and playing with the sounds we imitate or invent.

Gradually, *formative play* emerges, when children can distinguish between various toys, objects and materials. We begin to have

1

ideas of what we want to do and try to achieve these goals; that is, our play begins to have aim and direction. The child can also try to attain goals set by other people. By moving from *manipulation* to *formation* we begin to *create* and this creative activity is exciting and satisfying.

In the next stage of development, the child enters the world of *make-believe*. We begin to adopt personae, to act out roles; we test and explore social relationships and find ways of expressing our physical and creative abilities. By developing imaginary situations and acting out imaginary roles, the child escapes from the limitations of an every-day reality in which he or she is dependent and virtually powerless in an adult world. We are freed to develop fantasies that satisfy our needs, allowing us to be both actor and observer simultaneously. In occasional empathy with our playmates, we discover the intense pleasure that the shared experience has to offer.

Games with rules, which include all forms of sport, involve a change of emphasis. As children, we learn that if we want all the enjoyment that playing the game has to offer, we must adjust to a socially accepted, prearranged, set of rules. We voluntarily accept the discipline of the group, but discover that despite the loss of some personal freedom of choice, we gain the great satisfaction and fulfillment of group action. We also learn that playing can be hard work. (Unfortunately, the concomitant understanding that hard work can be fun is often rapidly destroyed by our school experience.) It is this form of play, of course, that we most consciously maintain throughout our adult life.

Thus, natural play performs a vital role in our physical and mental development and ideally it should help us to grow up with happy, healthy, well-rounded personalities. But the course of true play rarely does run smooth; numerous obstacles interfere with and distort the process.

Interference With Natural Play

During our formative years, our personalities are affected by environmental factors and pressures and by our attempts to adjust to, or circumvent them. We compete with our siblings for attention, we discover that the strong can bully the weak, the aggressive can dominate the timid; we learn to lie and we learn to manipulate. Our parents' behavior patterns form a major matrix for our development; whether our parents are understanding or muddled, rational, emotional, violent, prejudiced, loving or apathetic, or a mixture of all these things, we are unconsciously shaped by them. Deliberately or not, they will either stimulate or stultify our growth. "Young children," write Marzollo and Lloyd, "are exceptionally open to environmental influences. In a home where discovery is discouraged, children often learn how *not* to learn, a tragic outcome, to say the least." Indeed, for underprivileged children, parental and societal handicaps not only interfere with the development of play and distort its effects, but may even suppress some of its vital levels altogether.

As children and increasingly as adults, our play becomes a reflection and extension of our daily conflicts, frustrations and need for justification. We become more and more "result-oriented" and less and less "process-oriented." Thus, the fact that children often explode into violence or retreat into apathy when their creative energies are frustrated should surprise nobody.

Resistance to Change

Nobody today would admit to believing that learning is best achieved by the passive absorption of facts, concepts, and methods, to be regurgitated upon request. Yet for all the lip service paid to progressive ideas, our schools are still places where a good memory is the most highly valued of all talents. How many head teachers or inspectors have any real understanding of what is meant by creativity, or what it entails? I recently saw a letter to the head of a children's Center for Art, from the headmistress of a primary school. She complained that the children were being "allowed to scribble" and suggested they be taught how to draw "a recognizable dog."

Creative thought seems to threaten society since it leads to a questioning of the status quo and, thus, to demands for change. Perhaps, therefore, society ensures, consciously or not, that by bureaucratic means, large class sizes, rigid examination requirements, and so on, no real changes can be made. The inadequacy of governmental budget allocations is a wonderful excuse to do nothing. It is also true that simple inertia, a factor in any large system, is extremely difficult to overcome, even where good will is present.

What Is Creativity?

So far I have used the term creativity without attempting to define it, on the assumption that most readers will have some notion of what I have in mind. Few would argue with the concept of creativity as "the ability to originate, to bring into being" (*Webster's New World Dictionary*). What is less obvious is the answer to the question, "What creates creativity itself?" That is the question to which Arthur Koestler addresses himself in his seminal book *The Act of Creation*. He proposes that the act of creation occurs when one particular conceptual plane of thought meets or bisects another plane, and a hitherto unperceived association of ideas takes place. He suggests, for example, that virtually all forms of humor arise from this "bisociation," as he calls it. The most obvious example is the pun — a word that has more than one meaning, depending on its context, is used with one of its meanings in a second context where that meaning is inappropriate. If we are aware of the double meaning, we "see" the joke.

I believe that Koestler's point is well taken. Creativity thus springs from freedom and flexibility in associative thinking and from the ability to recognize that magic moment when two seemingly separate paths cross each other and briefly become one — that moment so powerfully exemplified in Archimedes' exultant "Eureka!" or Newton's flash of insight when down fell the apple. Of course, Koestler is not the only one to have recognized this principle, as the following two brief quotations show. But he is the one who developed the concept and formalized it in a book.

Research is to see what everybody else has seen, and to think what nobody else has thought. (Albert Szent-Gyorgyl)

Creativeness often consists of merely turning up what is already there. Did you know that right and left shoes were thought up little more than a century ago? (Bernice Fitz-Gibbon)

The Creativity of Play

It has been said that we "learn through experience and experiencing and it is very possible that what we call *talent* is simply a greater than average capacity for experiencing" (Viola Spolin, *Improvisation for the Theater*). This goes hand in hand with the bisociative concept of creativity described by Koestler. Also, truly creative people, in whatever field of endeavor, respond to the experience of living with some outward expression — they are driven to express themselves by the power of the experience. If, then, we help children to develop an individual capacity for experiencing as fully as possible, and to increase their flexibility and associative thinking, we shall help them develop a creative personality and increase their powers of self-expression.

4

Writing of imagination games, Richard de Mille writes, "We open up closed territory in the mind." Imagination games enable the child to

> think thoughts and visualize events that at first sight may seem forbidding. He learns that the domain of the imagination is larger and safer than he thought it was....We overcome the constricting effect of a too-great reliance upon what Freudians call "defense mechanisms." Protecting us from thinking thoughts that would provoke anxiety if fully formed in consciousness, defense mechanisms limit the degree of imagination available for creative use. *(Put Your Mother on the Ceiling)*

De Mille devised a series of games for parent or teacher and child that allow the child to learn, through experience, that the images and visions crowding in on one are actually the products of one's own imagination and thus, under one's own control. A good example of this was my own childhood terror of the monstrous faces I used to see in the abstract patterns of my bedroom curtains. If I lay facing them I was afraid to turn my back and if my back was toward the curtains, I was afraid to turn to face them. This situation continued for years and I needed a light on in the room, the door to the hall left open, and so on. Then one night, as a monster scowled at me from the curtains, a thought crossed my mind, "why do they never smile at me?" In that instant, the face smiled and in that instant I understood that the faces were all in my own head. The burden of years of fear fell away and from then on the curtains actually became a source of comfort and fascination. How sad that my parents, and those of countless generations of hapless children, never had the help of de Mille's book.

The use of games, then, can be seen to be crucially important in the child's development:

> The game is the natural group form providing the involvement and personal freedom necessary for experiencing. Personal techniques and skills are developed at the very moment a person is having all the fun and excitement playing a game has to offer — this is exactly the time he is truly open to receive them. *(Improvisation for the Theater)*

Let us say we wish to develop children's ability to concentrate. If we involve them fully in playing a game, simply enjoying the act of play as much as possible, they will naturally concentrate, within their current limits, without having to be reminded, or thinking about it. In fact, thinking about concentration *prevents* concentration. As we play game after game, our ability to concentrate should grow and become habitual, a natural part of our play and by extension, of our way of life.

When we play, we become personally involved and such involvement is essential to education, for true learning requires the discovery of meaning rather than the mere acquisition of knowledge.

Play for All Ages

In this introduction, I speak mostly to teachers with classes or groups of children of various ages. However, the games and exercises I describe can be incorporated into workshops and courses in creativity at virtually every age, up to and including the elderly. As I noted in the preface, I have worked with teachers and students, preschoolers, at risk and exceptional children, groups of foster parents, army officers in charge of cultural and educational activities, adults in evening classes, student teachers, pensioners, and kids at summer camp. Often, people of college age and upward are the most in need of developing their creative abilities.

The Advantages of Directed Play

Creativity games help properly trained teachers to encourage the development of positive qualities of character and mind in their pupils, while avoiding or counteracting the development of negative qualities. By the choice of game, selection of players, personal participation and intervention, and by the framework of explanation and discussion, the teacher enables the pupils to experience the fun and satisfaction that creative activity has to offer. This is also true of adult groups.

The players can begin to feel the enjoyment of, say, a shared activity; the more timid or at risk ones can be encouraged to take an active role, can feel the joy of having *their* suggestions adopted, and can discover that in these games they need have no fear of failure. There can be a great sense of release when children discover that there are times, even in the classroom, when it is fine to give their energies full rein, that they can jump, shout or sing, within the framework of the game, and that the greater the self-expression, the greater the satisfaction of all.

In such an atmosphere, children find out for themselves the value of different forms of activity; of the need to pay attention to one another, of the meaning of self-discipline. Teachers have reported that normally difficult classes have voluntarily spent lengthy periods in quiet, intense productivity, each sub-group working without continuous supervision on some problem inherent in the game. Discussions have revealed a growing understanding in the children of the world around them, of their relationship to it and to each other. The result — greater tolerance and mutual acceptance, greater self-confidence and enhanced curiosity and awareness.

We try to help the child develop qualities such as observation, a good memory (there's nothing wrong with a good memory — it just shouldn't be the only ability actually encouraged by the educational system), mental and physical relaxation, spontaneity, imagination, physical and mental integration, cooperation, and simple awareness.

People with these qualities will tend to be psychologically healthy and self-actualizing. They will become creative and valuable members of society, not by their unquestioning acceptance — or rejection — of prevalent values and concepts, but by their ability to see life afresh, to question, evaluate, and reformulate these values and concepts. They will be neither coldly analytical nor blindly emotional. The building of a society of such people is a vision worth striving for.

What I have said regarding children is equally true of other age groups. All can benefit from creativity workshops.

Mutual Advantage

A necessary prerequisite for the successful use of creative play in the classroom or workshop is that the teachers themselves must believe in the value of the games, have some necessary training, and be open and sensitive to the needs of their pupils. To try to use some of the games without adequate preparation, or personal belief in their efficacy, can be dangerous. Teachers have told me, for example, that a certain game was "useless, because the children didn't like it, didn't understand it and were bored." Yet, the same game had excellent results in comparable groups. I suspect that the teacher's own lack of understanding, and subsequent lack of ease and confidence, was transmitted to the class. Unless the teacher enjoys playing the game, it should be left alone. Some teachers have come to my workshops apparently willing to play, but wearing clothes that made true participation impossible—white slacks that couldn't be soiled, short skirts, and so on. In others, inhibitions have sometimes been revealed that prevented any meaningful participation in the games.

While there is a definite element of psychodrama in many of the games, unless the group leader has appropriate training, one should be wary of doing more than some consciousness raising. Certainly, no untoward pressure should be placed on group members to reveal more of themselves than they feel able to do. A cardinal rule in all workshops is that *the group has a collective responsibility to make every member feel as comfortable as possible and under no external pressure to "perform."*

In the vast majority of cases, however, playing can help the teacher just as much as playing can help the child. As the child develops positive qualities, so can the teacher. Reading about the games is not enough. Only by actually tackling them and facing the problems they pose can the necessary experience be gained. This is a rewarding experience in its own right. Let me quote from a personal letter I received from a remedial teacher who attended one of my courses:

> In my class I applied many of the exercises I learned in the workshop. My conceptions and approach changed. I came closer to my pupils; I played with them, enjoyed myself with them, understood them better and was thus able to help them with greater success.
>
> I learned something else in the workshops. I learned to play. I played with my pupils and they with me, and suddenly they discovered in me a friend, playing with them, *like* them. They saw me as flesh and blood, as one of them....And I sensed a full degree of trust which the children gave me, in a two-way flow of sympathy and love between us. This was an essential foundation for the educational and other activities I carried out to help my remedial class stride vigorously forward.

No system is foolproof and creative play, in and of itself, can work no miracles. The backbone of education remains the teacher-child relationship. Many pedagogical methods will show results for the sensitive, forceful teacher who can win the child's confidence and respect. No system, however advanced, can overcome the lack of such qualities.

At Risk Children

In the major part of this book I describe and discuss a wide range of games and exercises. I have drawn many of my illustrations from my work with children, from reactions and comments of students and teachers who have participated in my workshops in special education, and from reports by teachers who have applied some of the games in their remedial or other classes.

Very briefly, we distinguish between two main types of problem that bring children into remedial classes. First, there are those physiological disabilities that may be independent of the child's social background but interfere with the learning processes. Disabilities, such as dyslexia or cerebral palsy, that cause difficulties of coordination, articulation, aphasia, hearing problems, and so on, can cause problems in reading and writing, memory, body image, and physical and mental integration. Most important of all, they can intensify psychological insecurity and a sense of uselessness. In conjunction with other forms of therapy, creative games have proved their success in combating such problems, letting the children express themselves at their own level, helping them discover hidden abilities, and building self-confidence.

The second type of problem is emotional or cultural in origin. Here again, games can help the teacher to create the right kind of positive, cooperative atmosphere that can break down barriers, reduce suspicion, antagonism, and fear, and answer the child's desperate need for attention, all of which can destroy the learning process. Moreover, modern research suggests direct environmental causes for many of the learning disabilities of at risk children and points to the use of play as a useful way of tackling the problem (See Smilansky, *The Effects of Sociodramatic Play on Disadvantaged Preschool Children*).

Exceptional Children

No less than at risk children, exceptional children can also benefit greatly from creative play. First, they have usually learned how to succeed in the competitive world of the upper percentiles of the school system. This means that they may be quite self-centered and unused to cooperating with others, sometimes tending to view them, either as potential rivals, or as hardly worthy of much attention or respect. Second, although they are good processors of information, this can mean that they are often highly left-brain oriented. The result can be a child who is clever but not particularly wise, who is used to receiving the plaudits of the surrounding adults and has become intellectually just a little arrogant.

However, when I teach exceptional kids, either in special groups, or as part of a regular group, I usually note that after a short period of suspicion and reserve, they are bright enough to grasp the concepts I am offering them. While they still tend to be overly critical, both of the games and the efforts of the group, they quickly become enthusiastic as an entirely new world of experiences opens up to them. It can also be a salutary revelation to them when children they regard as their intellectual inferiors prove to be their creative and imaginative equals, and may even outshine them in some respects. While they may be used to some of their peers outplaying them in sports, they expect to win at anything smacking of a "thought" game. Not infrequently, I have seen them go away with a new respect for other children, and a greater appreciation of a sharing comradeship.

Clearly, any child can benefit from developing creative and imaginative abilities, and in this sense, exceptional children have much to gain.

Conclusion

Theatre Games embodies a pragmatic, rather than a dogmatic, approach to a humanistic educational process. As teachers and group leaders begin to use games techniques and ideas, discover variations and applications, and begin to report on their successes and failures, the greater will be our ability to apply the lessons learned. It is to be hoped that teachers will be motivated to exchange experiences and to pool their knowledge. A group of remedial teachers who started meeting regularly in the wake of one of my workshops, told me how their individual sense of isolation, often the result of being the only remedial teacher in their school, had been dissipated.

It has been shown that any group — from kindergarteners to pensioners, from prison inmates to exceptional children — can benefit from games like those described in this book. But these notes represent only a tentative step forward on a long and thorny road. It is a road that can lead us toward the development of a powerful educational tool; a tool that shall help us to see ourselves and to see one another a little more honestly and clearly, a tool that can help us release some of the immense potential lying dormant in the human spirit.

THE GAMES

You can do anything with children if only you play with them.
Prince Otto von Bismarck

In every real man a child is hidden that wants to play.
Friedrich Nietzsche

GROUP ORIENTATION

The deepest need of man, then, is the need to overcome his
separateness, to leave the prison of his aloneness.

Eric Fromm, *The Art of Loving*

Face to Face

This exercise is of particular value for the orientation of a
group of adults or older children at the very beginning of a series of
workshops. It helps to introduce the participants to each other and
introduces them to a central problem.

The players arrange themselves in two rows, facing each other
in pairs. Then the partners are asked simply to look at
each other for a minute or two, quietly concentrating
on this basic action. Fidgeting, embarrassed
giggles, whispers and other signs of tension and loss of concentration soon
appear. This is more noticeable with partners who are strangers to each other, but
is surprisingly evident even where the
partners are good friends.

Subsequent discussion reveals some
shock that an apparently simple exercise
can prove so difficult, although sometimes people showing signs of great tension declare that they have found no difficulty at all. Others will object that the
exercise is quite artificial, since it is not
natural for people to look at each other
so openly, or that it is "rude to stare." As
the discussion continues, the players are
led to consider the fact that in our particular society, we just do not
look at other people deeply, and are disturbed by others looking
deeply at us. The question arises, "Why should this be?" In other
societies this is not necessarily the norm. A friend who spent some
years in Zambia told me that there, staring at people is considered

a sign of friendliness and welcome; people will cross the street to look at a stranger with no embarrassment on either side.

Exchanging Names

The *Face to Face* exercise is renewed and when a greater degree of relaxation is felt, the couples are asked to exchange names; I tell you my name and you tell me yours, without shyness or whispering. This is a simple act, but it symbolizes a sense of sharing, of openness. Given our modern sense of alienation, it is no wonder that so often we are introduced to somebody and two minutes later have quite forgotten the person's name. One student told me with some amazement, however, that after taking part in this exercise, she now remembers the names of students with whom she has attended classes "for ages," but whose names she could never remember. Other players confirmed this experience.

Depending on the size of the group and the time available, players should switch partners, until each has "met" all the others. It is also good for the leader to take part in this process.

Cue Names

For younger children, this is an excellent name-learning game that also aids memory development. The children sit in a circle on chairs or on the floor and the teacher chooses one child to begin. The child makes a physical gesture, such as clapping hands, pulling an ear, circling, or any other gesture that he or she thinks of, and at the same time says his or her name. The next child in the circle repeats the gesture and the name and then adds a new gesture, together with his or her own name. Thus, each child, in turn, repeats the gestures and names of all those who came before.

The process is repeated till all the children have taken part. When a child has difficulty remembering the sequence, the other children in the circle help out and you often find that most of the children join spontaneously in the chanting of the names and the repetition of the gestures. The group concentration can be remarkable. Again, it is good for the teacher to join the circle and take a turn with the others. This shows the children that the teacher is prepared to make the effort with them and if the teacher makes a mistake, the children have great fun correcting it. It also helps the teacher to remember the names of all the children.

You and Me

Here is a good icebreaker, reported to me by a high school teacher who attended one of my courses. She works with teenagers and has found that the exercise works well, even with kids who don't yet know each other.

The group divides into pairs, either by arbitrary selection, or by the players choosing partners. Each partner has to tell the other something about themselves, freely choosing whatever he or she considers important or appropriate. After a few minutes, the children take turns relating the information to the rest of the group. There may be whispered consultations, with one asking the other things like, "Is it all right if I tell them *such and such?*" Sometimes, we see intimate smiles, and a sense of comradeship and sharing can be the result. Indeed, it is not uncommon for pairs to become friends, but the sense of sharing is not confined to the couples, since everybody has had some of his or her private life and thoughts presented openly to the whole group. The game has an added bonus: because the partners know they are going to have to remember the details told them, in order to repeat them to the others, a high degree of concentration can usually be observed.

Exercises

- Do you know another "introduction" game or exercise? Write it down. Explain it to the instructor or to the group and see how it works.

- Think of a variation for one of the exercises described above, or an extra stage.

UNIT 2:
TRUST

...the most fundamental prerequisite of mental vitality is a sense of basic trust.

Erik Erikson, *Identity*

Introduction

Having discovered, in group orientation activities, that it is really rather difficult to "give and take," we can now set about building a sense of group trust. In order for each of us to feel free to tackle each game in a personal, open way, we must first feel that the other players will support us positively, that each attempt at self-expression will be encouraged and that the egotistical needs of the others will not lead them to abandon us or undermine our efforts. If we are to take a courageous, imaginative leap into the unknown, we must know that our partners will help us to fly. The space where we are playing must become a magic place, where everything is permitted — except destructive criticism.

It seems that whenever we see something new, or hear a suggestion or a proposal, our first instinct is to look for what's *wrong* with it. This naturally creates a negative atmosphere, since the person criticized is put on the defensive and will be disinclined to accept one's own contributions in turn. Therefore, comments on someone else's actions should always begin with praise for the good aspects of the work. All too often, a good idea is nipped in the bud because it does not emerge complete and in full bloom, but peeps forth tentatively, partly formed. Shortcomings are at once seized upon, the idea is discarded and whatever fruitful germ of creativity it contained is lost. Similarly, in creativity exercises, it is very counterproductive to concentrate on the failure of a player to fulfill all the requirements of the game.

The question therefore arises: how do we achieve a positive atmosphere? How do we learn to trust our fellow players? There is no easy trick that can create mutual emotional trust. Such trust must be earned and is the result of good will and application. A good way to start this process, however, is to concentrate on games involving *physical* trust, since these require less overt emotional commitment

17

and can be learned as a technique.

Catch Me Falling

A group of six or seven players forms a rather tight circle, with one player in the center. Those in the circle stand with one foot behind the other, with their knees slightly bent, and with their arms extended toward the center player. He (or she) then allows himself to fall backward, to be gently cushioned on the hands of those standing behind him. They restore him to an upright position and he then allows himself to fall forward. By shifting his heels slightly, he gradually moves round the circle. The players then change places until all have been in the center.

Although this game seems to be purely physical, it has emotional aspects. Many of us find it difficult to rely on anybody but ourselves. Some players may show great resistance or fear and be unable to let themselves fall, giving various excuses (wrong shoes, too heavy), but gradually this resistance can be overcome. It can usually be demonstrated that even the smallest and lightest player, having learned the correct method of support, can hold up the tallest or heaviest person in the group. If necessary, the circle can be tightened and the degree of falling lessened. Those in the circle must work together to make the one in the middle feel safe. Even a momentary distraction can cause unreadiness, and the faller often falls toward the space between two catchers, who must therefore work together. That is their responsibility. Indeed, it is the responsibility of everyone in the circle, including those on the opposite side, to ensure the faller's security. On the other hand, it is the faller's responsibility to accept the others' support; we must learn to place our trust in the group and they must earn that trust. Then the circle can be widened and the degree of falling can be increased. I have seen students achieve a remarkable degree of confidence, really flinging themselves backward, to be saved inches from the floor. When the game is working well, players often comment on a wonderful sense of freedom and well-being, of being "looked after" by the others. This can happen even at a first session between people who have only just met.

18

The game has been very successful with children, even in remedial classes. One teacher reported that a boy in her class, antagonistic and disruptive and rejected by the others, took part in the game reluctantly, claiming that the other children would deliberately let him fall because "they hate me." After his turn in the center (his eyes having been closed) he insisted that only the teacher had supported him, she moving round the circle to catch him each time. The game was then repeated and this time she moved to the other side of the room. When he opened his eyes, he realized that the other children had indeed supported him and "a shy smile crossed his face." This then led to a class discussion of his problems and after that his relations with his classmates improved just a little.

Tossing

Six or eight players face each other in two lines and they link their hands together to create a flat, horizontal lattice-work of arms. This support becomes a flexible launching pad to flip a person into the air. With a minimum of experimentation you will find the best system to join arms. Be careful when joining arms that the bend of elbows goes with the movement of the body returning from the throw. Grasping each other at the wrists provides the best hold.

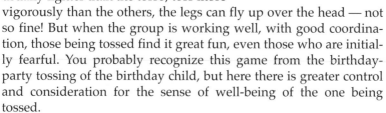

Once the human litter of hands is formed another player lies down, face up, across the linked hands. Working together, the players begin to raise and lower him with increasing force, until he is being lightly tossed clear of their hands. Cooperation and coordination are paramount. If, for example, the couple supporting the legs, which are usually lighter than the torso, toss more vigorously than the others, the legs can fly up over the head — not so fine! But when the group is working well, with good coordination, those being tossed find it great fun, even those who are initially fearful. You probably recognize this game from the birthday-party tossing of the birthday child, but here there is greater control and consideration for the sense of well-being of the one being tossed.

Yo Heave Ho

This is a development of *Tossing*, suitable for large groups of fifteen players or more. They form two lines facing each other and link hands as before. One player goes to the end of the line and this time lies face *down* on the linked arms, with his own arms stretching forward. A second player goes to the other end of the line and waits. The group now starts a backward and forward swaying motion, until the "cargo" is being heaved along with each forward sway. When he reaches the other end, the second player takes his hands and helps to swing him clear. Care should be taken to remove troublesome items that can get caught, like watches, or pens in breast pockets. When all goes well, there are great scenes of joint effort and hilarity.

Leading the Blind

The players split up into threes. One of the three closes his eyes while the other two take him by the hands and lead him around the room, around obstacles, into the corridor, up and down stairs or wherever there is available space. The leaders must explain verbally any difficulties to be encountered. Then the roles are switched. Although this sounds easy, a fair amount of initial fear or resistance is often experienced. The leaders, too, find that cooperation and concentration are required, if the one being led is not to be confused. Where necessary, of course, the game can be played in pairs.

Good results were reported from one remedial class of second and third graders. Although timid children found it hard to walk freely with their eyes closed, and needed to "peep" now and then, the class as a whole enjoyed the game and asked to play it again. One boy said that being conducted and looked after by others made him "feel like a king." The children themselves devised further variations, such as joining hands in a line, with only the front child leading and guiding the others. The teacher also told me that she subsequently saw them playing the game in the playground — a sure sign that the game had given them satisfaction. It should be noted that the need to explain what was happening to the "blind" child also provided important practice in verbalization: "We're turning left. There's a step up just in front of us."

A second teacher, when she asked her pupils to describe what they felt like or saw when their eyes were closed, was told by one little girl that she saw a terrible giant coming to eat her up. The teacher then found out that the girl suffered from many hidden fears, nightmares, bed-wetting, and so on. Naturally, this information was of great use in the further handling of the child. It is clear that these games can be of considerable diagnostic value and the alert teacher can pick up useful insights.

Another teacher tried the following variation:

Leading by a String

Each child holds one end of a long piece of string or rope, while another child holds all the other ends. By pulling gently, the leader guides each child in turn, eyes closed, towards him or her. Various obstacles, a chair, a table, box or schoolbag, are placed in the way; and the leader must warn them and tell them how to avoid the obstacles.

Fingertips

The players work in pairs. They touch fingertips, all ten fingers. One player then closes his eyes and the other player leads him around the room, turning and swooping, now slow, now fast, kneeling, sitting down, climbing over things and making the actions as varied as possible, without breaking fingertip contact. He must keep his "blind" partner from tripping or bumping into things or colliding with other couples. As the blind partner gains confidence and trust, he will become more venturesome. It is, in fact, the blind partner who governs the tempo, since if the leader moves too rapidly, contact cannot be maintained. Each partner must concentrate, responding to the other's rhythms and impulses. After a while, they exchange roles. Simpler forms of the game can be devised for younger children, or those with disabilities.

Blind Running

This is also played in pairs or trios. The sighted partners grasp the blind one firmly by the hand and start to run, first at a slow trot and then gradually building up speed. Naturally, this takes place in the corridor, or out in the yard. The same concentration and attention is required as in *Fingertips*, and the blind partner's trust must be earned. He, for his part, must "push through" his fear. After a while, the roles are switched.

As in other games of this type, a warning must be sounded. Children are often thoughtless or cruel, and those in remedial (and even regular) classes can have emotional problems. It may happen that they try to exploit games of this type to deliberately cause another pupil to fall, and therefore these games require careful supervision. This does not imply that they cannot be used, but, perhaps, at the start, pairs or threes should work in sequence rather than all at the same time, thus allowing the teacher to observe each group separately.

Solitaire

The group spreads out along both sides of a corridor or other lengthy space. With closed eyes, one player runs from one end of the space to the other. The others guard him from danger, prevent him from straying to the left or right and catch him gently at the end. If running proves too difficult, a firm walk can be substituted, and running achieved later on.

This game can be amazingly difficult. After even a few steps, the sense of a wall looming up in front of you is powerful and one must force oneself to continue, even though it is perfectly clear that the others will protect one from harm. This is an excellent metaphoric example of the kind of defensive wall we erect around ourselves that, by inhibiting us unnecessarily, prevents our creative energy from finding outlets in shared experiences. These exercises improve group trust in another way: they give the players a sense of personal difficulty that is openly demonstrated and shared by all. As one student said of *Solitaire*, "It looked so easy that I laughed to myself at the fear and hesitation of the others. Then, when it was my turn, I found I was just as scared." Children often have difficulty understanding, or even conceiving of, points of view other than their own. Thus, these games, in which they switch roles from leader to led, from sight to blindness, help them to gain insight, without the need for explanation. They simply *experience* two points of view in juxtaposition.

Note: These games should not be used just at the beginning of a course or series of workshops and then forgotten. They should be repeated from time to time. It is interesting to see how great a degree of group trust can be developed. An improvisational group, of which I was a member, eventually reached a point when we were able to run about with closed eyes on the flat roof of the building in which we rehearsed. We had real confidence that no one would allow us to fall off the edge — and we lived to tell the tale!

Exercises

• Can you think of another "trust" game or exercise? Write it down. Explain it to the instructor or to the group and see how it works.

22

- Think of a variation for one of the exercises described above, or an additional stage.

- Write a description of what it feels like to be "blind."

- How many different ways can you think of to complete the following sentences:

"Trusting the other players is as hard as _____."

"Trusting the other players is as easy as _____."

UNIT 3:
WARMING UP

"Warm up...to practice or exercise a while before going into a game...to make or become more animated, excited, ardent, enthusiastic, lively."
Webster's New World Dictionary

Introduction

In virtually every sphere of activity involving the use of the body, the necessity of physically warming up is recognized and it is obvious that mental and bodily preparation go hand in hand. For the sportsman, the opera singer, or the concert pianist, warming up is second nature. Yet most of us go through our daily activities without any kind of preparation at all. As a result, we are rarely fully alert or totally concentrated. Worries, expectations, and other problems invade our thoughts at the most inappropriate times and we are physically tense, inhibited and imbalanced. Happily, there is a growing awareness of the need for mental and physical fitness, but we've still a long way to go.

In group work, warm-ups are particularly important. The workshop needs to be a special place in which anything becomes possible. The players must become habituated to individual preparation. It is not within the scope of this book to explore this aspect of physical education in any depth, so I shall content myself with suggesting that as the players arrive they should quietly find an unoccupied part of the playing area and do a few stretching, relaxation, and breathing exercises. These help us to concentrate on ourselves for a short while, locate areas of stiffness, and re-enter the workshop atmosphere.

With younger children, these simple physical exercises should be directed by the teacher, with everybody standing in a large circle.

When everybody is present, group warm-ups can begin.

Note: In this book, I have placed this chapter after *Trust*, because I feel that in the very first session of a group workshop, the building of group trust is paramount. However, after the first one or two meetings, warming up should always be the *first* stage in any workshop.

Let's Play Tag

Playing tag is an excellent way of warming up a group of players prior to proceeding to other games. The sheer fun of the thing helps people forget the outside world for a bit and recaptures their youthful spirit of play. It encourages the intimate, free atmosphere needed for proper communication. It also warms the players up physically and allows the body to forget the inhibitions of everyday manners and life. It is also a perfect example of the game which involves conflict through cooperation. The player who avoids being tagged by hiding outside the playing area cannot be said to "win" the game, since that player does not really participate in the game at all. Players quickly come to understand that the real fun lies in testing the limits of reasonable risk — how close can one come to the tagger without attracting attention? It also requires much concentration to know who the tagger is at every moment.

Slow-Motion Tag

Preparatory Exercise: The players walk individually around the playing area. The director calls out, "Walk faster...walk slower... slow-motion walk." The players then try to slow down their walk, imitating a movie run in slow motion. They become aware of the way their bodies move; they discover just how unconscious they normally are of their own bodily functions. As we try to continue to move, we often discover that we have forgotten *how* to move. Natural actions, such as swinging the arms in opposition to the legs, become uncoordinated. Exaggerated, parodic movements replace simplicity. A little practice, however, helps most players focus on their actions and rediscover natural motion. We now play *Tag* again.

After a couple of minutes of regular tag, the teacher calls out, "Slow motion!" The players continue the game without a pause, but instantly slow down. The aim remains the same as before — to play tag, but now in slow motion. Of course, one cannot actually duplicate running and jumping in slow motion because the laws of gravity prevail, but much of the feel of the thrust and rhythm of the movement can be retained. Note, also, that if you are about to be tagged, you cannot escape by making a sudden movement, breaking the convention of slow motion. Nor can the tagger shoot out a hand to catch an escaping player. Or rather, I should say that the hand *may* shoot out, but only in slow motion.

The game can be vastly entertaining, with players making extraordinary efforts to catch and avoid each other. There is genuine tension generated as the tagger's hand j-u-s-t f-a-i-l-s to contact the slowly twisting back of a prospective victim, or as the prey's face slowly registers alarm, horror and finally resignation as the hand approaches with the inevitability of a Greek tragedy.

During the game, the teacher, while participating, should remind the group to "breathe in slow motion, laugh in slow motion, groan in slow motion."

Note: Slow motion can be incorporated into most games involving physical activity. For instance in *Play Ball* (see the section on *Reality Games*) it can be useful if the players are having trouble visualizing the ball or catching it with a full body reaction.

One-Time Tag

This version can be played at either normal or slow motion speeds. Once a player has used, say, the right hand to tag somebody, that hand can no longer be used for tagging. One by one the limbs are "used up" so that the players must employ more and more outlandish parts of the body. Elbows, knees, toes, belly, buttocks, hair, ears, tongue — all come into play. Not being able to use the hands forces the players to use their bodies more imaginatively and helps overcome inhibitions, encouraging intimacy and lack of restraint. It is impossible to remain impersonal while licking your victim.

One teacher gave a warning that this version is not to be recommended with unruly children. She had a terrible time calming them down afterward, and one girl in her class used her teeth!

Kitty in the Corner

This is a well-known children's game. Depending on the size and shape of the playing area, four or six players choose "corners" and stand in them while a further player stands in the middle. The players must make eye contact with one another and exchange places, while the one in the middle attempts to capture a corner.

The players should be as adventurous as possible, crossing on the diagonal as well as switching places with neighbors. They should actively seek out eye contacts and keep on the move. This calls for attention and concentration, and the faster the pace, the greater the excitement. The most frequent cause of a player losing a corner is trying to exchange places with another player without proper eye contact. The second player fails to respond and the hapless runner is stranded in the middle. Groan, curse, giggle!

It is possible to play *Kitty in the Corner* in slow motion, but the middle player will be caught out less easily since one's reaction time ceases to play a part.

Exercises

• Do you know another warm-up game or exercise? Write it down. Explain it to the instructor or to the group and see how it works.

• Think of a variation for one of the exercises described above, or an extra stage.

• Think of other games in which you have to "take risks" in order to enjoy the game fully. Tell the group your idea.

UNIT 4:
DEVELOPING THE SENSES

The greatest thing a human soul ever does in this world is to see something, and tell what it saw in a plain way. Hundreds of people can talk for one who can think, but thousands can think for one who can see. To see clearly is poetry, prophecy, and religion, all in one.

John Ruskin

Introduction

In this modern, noisy, aggressive world, we have a tendency to protect ourselves by shutting it out. Glaring advertisements, raucous music, and the mass media, bombard us at every turn, and our senses have become dulled. Like drug users needing ever greater doses to achieve their "high," we need stronger and stronger sensory stimulation to make an impression on us — so much so that teenagers have their hearing permanently impaired by their literally deafening entertainment. In this way they demonstrate, both symbolically and practically, their profound alienation from society. But very few of us either hear, see, smell, feel, or taste, to the fullest of our capabilities. Our contact with reality is thereby weakened. In order to feel more at home in our environment, and to experience it more fully, we must rediscover its always fresh fascination. We can start this process by sharpening our benumbed senses — by literally opening our eyes.

The Amazing Classroom

At first sight, few classrooms are particularly stimulating spaces. Tedious and standardized in shape, decoration, and furnishing, they are at best regarded as neutral environments, even when teachers attempt to brighten them up with pupils' art work or posters. It is our eye that is at fault. In this game, the group is asked to look around the classroom and count the number of splashes of, say, the color red. Often there are surprisingly many to be found: part of a plastic electrical fitting, the cover of a book, part of a wall poster, a piece of chalk, a stain on a desk — the list grows. Half a dozen or more items in a moderately sized room is not unusual. Now we do the same for green, brown, black, yellow, gray, white and metallic shades. Again we find that they abound. We have discovered that this apparently dull room is actually filled with color — and we haven't even included the clothes we are wearing.

Now let us look for geometric figures and shapes: circles, squares, oblongs, triangles, curves, and patterns. Again we find that the room is crammed with interest.

The same applies to the variety of materials to be found: wood, plastics, plaster, ceramics, metals, cloth, glass, paint, concrete, paper, chalk…! Countless lessons in the sciences and the arts could be based just on the structure and contents of the room.

What has happened? The room itself has not changed, but our way of looking at it has. Through the medium of a simple exercise, our eyes have been opened. If, by conscious choice, we repeat the exercise whenever we find ourselves with a minute to spare in a room — waiting at the dentist or in a government office, for example — we can help this new awareness to become habitual and instinctive. As our powers of observation grow and we experience the richness of the world around us, our lives will be enriched.

This is the primary function of the game. For adults, there is a secondary function. We become aware of our "normal" level of sensory awareness and this new consciousness can help us in our efforts to become more self-actualizing.

In education, the game can help young or at risk children learn the names of things, distinguish colors, count or remember, and can even provide useful exercises in reading, writing, or drawing.

Through Other Eyes

This is not strictly a sensory development exercise, but it is closely related to *The Amazing Classroom* and does call for close observation. Another way to look at a familiar room or environment is to imagine that you are some other person with a quite different background. How would a tribesman from the jungles of Borneo experience the same place? How would a person from the middle ages experience it? The Secretary of Education? A child on his first day at school? A blind person? Such questions force us to re-examine our perceptions of an environment and to realize how subjective our reactions are. At the same time, the game can be a fascinating experience for children as they try to imagine themselves in someone else's skin, and gives rise to a host of questions about the way of life of the "subject."

Exercises

• Choose another "boring" place, and repeat the above two games.

• Suggest another person or kind of person who might react differently to the classroom.

Listen to the Birdie

The players sit quietly for a minute or so, listening to the sounds in the environment and trying to identify them. The players then compare the sounds heard: birds, traffic, breathing, creaking chairs, far-off voices. Most players remark on the wide range of sounds to be heard, sounds of which we are normally unaware, since, not being in the focus of our attention, they are filtered out of our consciousness.

While this is essentially an exercise in sensory awareness, it also helps develop other capabilities, such as concentration and memory, all the more so if we must remember all the sounds and list them after the listening period is over. With practice, players should be able to distinguish between similar sounds. How many *kinds* of birds can be heard? Is that a bus or a truck in the road outside? Are those the footsteps of a man or a woman in the corridor?

One teacher found the game valuable in several ways. Her class of five- and six-year-olds was normally noisy and difficult to control, but during the game they kept really quiet and tried to listen. The game helped them to identify and name the sources of sounds, increasing the children's vocabulary and their descriptive ability. The teacher asked questions such as, "What is the difference between the sound of a bus and the sound of a car?" or, "What is the difference between the banging of a hammer and a door?" Another teacher asked her class to "become" the things they heard. One by one they pantomimed a bird, a workman, a car, with the others joining in the pantomime when they identified what was being acted out.

In yet another variation, the teacher concealed herself behind a board and created her own noises which the class had to identify. She jingled keys and then coins, scratched and then tapped on the board, made popping sounds, and so on. Then, each child had a turn to hide and invent their own sounds for the class to hear. Great fun was had by all.

Exercises

- List some other items that can be identified by the sounds they make.

Recalling a Sound

The players sit quietly and each one tries to recall a particular sound and recreate it as fully as possible in the imagination. The aim here is not to describe the sound, but simply to hear it again as clearly as possible.

In one of my university classes, a student suddenly got up during the exercise and left the room briefly. When she returned she explained that she had tried to remember the sound of a solo violin work by Bach and was astounded to hear a student in the music academy next door practicing that very work. Leaving the room to find the source of the sound, she was even more astounded to discover that the sound had been totally in her head all along. I myself have had a similar experience. Unable to sleep one night, I tried to imagine the sound of bells and became convinced that bells were, in fact, tolling in a church some distance away. When I went out onto the balcony to hear them better, I discovered that I had been imagining them.

This seems to be an aural form of what is known as *eidetic imagery*, usually described as a visual phenomenon. An eidetic image is so vivid that it is almost indistinguishable from something actually seen or heard. There is some evidence that such imagery is particularly present in young children and in creative adults; Hogarth, Blake, Charlotte Brontë, Dickens, Thackeray, Daudet, Shelley, Coleridge and Edward Elgar all made statements suggesting the presence and use of eidetic images. The case of William Blake is particularly relevant, since it seems that he was able to evoke such images at will and even taught his wife to do so as well. Thus, when he drew a picture of an imaginary figure, such as his "Soul of a Flea," all he had to do was to use his imagination to create an eidetic image. He then simply drew the figure he was actually seeing in front of him, just as he would have done with a live model.

Whether it can be proven or not, I think it probable that there is a connection between this rich sensory perception and a creative inner life. If we can help our children to retain and develop their vivid sensory abilities, we shall surely be encouraging their creativity; if we can manage to recapture our own lost perception, we shall enrich our own lives.

I Remember It Well

The group sits quietly for a few minutes and each player tries to remember some event in the past with as much clarity and detail as possible. It could be a basketball game, a visit to the beach, a museum, a wedding, or simply sitting in a sidewalk cafe. Remember the colors, the sounds, the sights, smells and movements. What images are particularly vivid? Occasionally a player is surprised and delighted to remember some detail which had not impressed him or her at the time: the color of a woman's dress; the feel of drops of water on the face when someone splashed in the swimming pool nearby.

For children and, indeed, players of all ages, there is a simple variation. First of all the teacher asks the children to "hear," "see," "smell," "feel," or "taste" some familiar thing, using their imagination. Hear a motor car. See a red ball. Smell fresh bread. Feel a piece of wet soap. Taste a banana. Then each child is given a turn at choosing the next item and to say if it is to be heard, seen, smelled, felt or tasted.

Yum-Yum

Each player thinks of something simple to eat, such as ice cream, corn-on-the-cob, cake, or an apple. The player now proceeds to eat the food, concentrating on the taste, smell, texture, and so on.

Note that the object of the game is not to "act out" the eating, so that the others can guess what the food is, but to concentrate on recreating the sensations involved. This rule applies to any action performed involving the imagination. When players direct their attention outward, "telling" the others rather than concentrating inwardly on simply "doing," the results are usually artificial, exaggerated and unconvincing. This is so because in directing one's attention outward and in trying to "explain" one's actions to the audience, the player forgets to "feel" and tends to fall back on stereotyped or symbolic gestures that take the place of real actions.

This game creates great merriment, as players indulge themselves in their favorite delicacies and exchange ribald comments on their respective eating habits.

The teacher aids the process by asking questions as the game proceeds: How hard do you have to chew? What does it feel like when you swallow? Is it sticky, wet, hot, dry, or spicy? The players must make sure that whatever they are eating has substance. For instance, if you are eating a chicken leg, the fingers of the hand holding it can't be pressed together, since the bone would get in the way. You must feel the bone between the fingers.

Several teachers have told me of the game's success in the classroom. On one occasion, the children made a group decision to eat hamburgers. One child became the short-order cook, slapping the meat on the grill, toasting the rolls and adding fried onions. The others ordered, paid, helped themselves to mustard, relish, ketchup, or salt, and munched away with a will.

Exercises

• Suggest and try out another eating activity that can be performed by the whole group.

What Am I Holding?

The teacher assembles a variety of small everyday objects and conceals them from the players in a bag. I use my "bag of tricks"

that I describe in the section on *Transformation, Discovery and Spontaneity*. With adults, each player can contribute some article from a pocket or handbag, such as a key ring, a pen, a brooch or a cigarette lighter. Players take a turn standing with their backs to the group and are handed an item behind their backs. The player must try to identify the object and is asked to describe it as minutely as possible, trying to include every detail. The player must try to pin down just why, for example, he thinks the pen is plastic rather than metal; she thinks the purse is leather rather than plastic; it feels old rather than new; and suggests what color it is.

The game tries to redevelop those senses normally subordinated to sight. If a blindfold is used, the articles can be handled in front of the face and can be smelled or rubbed against the cheek. Players often comment that familiar objects, even when successfully identified, feel strange and give a sense of being larger or smaller than one remembers.

Children of many ages enjoy the game and it is of value in

developing the senses, sense memory, vocabulary, and descriptive powers. Phrases such as "a sort of sharp thing," can be investigated and the teacher, by asking relevant questions, can help the children express themselves with greater clarity and precision.

Feel-Fast

This variation was developed by a remedial teacher for her second and third grade classes. Two children sit opposite each other at a table. Behind each child is a box containing ten objects, such as chalk, a rubber band, a coin or a pencil. Each child is also given ten cards with the names and/or pictures of the objects depicted on them. The children look at the first card and then feel in the box behind them till they find the appropriate object, which they now place on the table. If the object is wrong, they replace it and try again. They then look at the second card, and so on. The game can be played with or without a time limit and after the round is over they try to remember the names of as many objects as they can, either by telling the class, or by writing them on the board.

Children with learning disabilities, who had difficulty finding the right objects, improved markedly as the game was repeated, identifying more than twice as many items correctly as they had before. Similarly, a girl with a memory problem, who could remember no more than five items at the beginning, improved her score to ten by the end, even though the objects in the box were changed from time to time.

It will be noted that this game can contain an element of competition, but need not do so. It is possible to make the children feel that the real competition is with themselves and their previous scores. The teacher can maintain a record, showing each child's individual achievements. Thus, children who are outscored by a partner can feel satisfaction if their own scores have improved, or they have finished their turn in less time than before.

An even simpler variation of the game has the children spread out the cards, select objects from the box, and then match the object with the corresponding card. Thus, word acquisition and recognition go hand in hand with sensory development, while the children have the fun of playing an exciting game.

I Feel Me

The players sit quietly, or move quietly around the playing space and, at the teacher's direction, begin to concentrate on various

35

parts of the body, starting with the toes and working up, or moving at random from one part to another. They are asked to feel the toes inside the socks; feel the toe muscles flexing; feel the small of the back; feel the eyelashes; feel the tips of the fingers; feel the weight of your body as it presses on the sole of the foot.

What happens here is that we suddenly focus on sense information we are actually receiving all the time, but either relegate to the background or filter out as unimportant. To use the terms of Gestalt Therapy, the feeling in the toes emerges from the "ground" to become the "figure," returning to the "ground" as we transfer our focus elsewhere.

The proponents of Gestalt Therapy believe that in the healthy personality there is ease and flexibility in the movement between "figure" and "ground." Lack of such flexibility, with an image refusing to leave the focus of attention, is indicative of rigidity or fixation, while lack of figure formation is indicative of repression. The assumption of Perls, Hefferline and Goodman, in their book *Gestalt Therapy*, is that average people, raised in an atmosphere full of splits, have lost their integrity and wholeness and suffer from incomplete gestalt formation. The authors, in a series of experiments — actually games (!) — offer therapeutic techniques to heal the dualism and help the person function as a whole. They place great stress on sensory contact with the environment. Indeed, the very first four of their experiments come under the general heading of "Contacting the Environment."

Space Walk

This game is an extension of *I Feel Me*. The players again move quietly around the room, becoming aware of the space and of themselves moving in and through it. They feel themselves "penetrating" the space, letting the whole body contact it. As they move around, they again focus on specific parts of the body, either on their own initiative, or at the teacher's direction. They feel the air as it flows into the nostrils, the roots of the hair, the shoulders rubbing against the shirt. At this stage, players work entirely alone, conscious of the other players only insofar as they take care not to "break in" to the other players' spaces.

Wading

This exercise is a development of *Space Walk*, with the addition of a further dimension. As the players move through the playing space, the teacher or director tells them that the nature of the space is changing. It is becoming heavier, thicker, and more difficult to penetrate. It is as if the air were changing to fog, to heavy mist, to water, oil, mud, tar and finally, to hardening concrete. The players push their way through it, feeling the ever greater effort needed, feeling the space pressing on the eyeballs, the lungs, the top of the head, until all movement becomes impossible. Then, at the teacher's direction, a progressive lightening begins. Now the players can take a step backward and look at the shapes they have left in the space, can look at the paths they have carved through it. As the space continues to lighten, the players feel themselves becoming freer, breathing more easily. By the end of the exercise, the sense of release can be exhilarating.

This game helps to develop sense memory. One might object that few of us have actually experienced wading through hardening concrete, but it is here that the imagination comes into play, taking genuine sense memories and applying and extending them to situations we have not yet experienced. This process is at the heart of an actor's training. How many of us have actually experienced, say, being strangled to death? But the actress playing Desdemona must do exactly that. On a less extreme level, the game, by incorporating an imaginative element into the sensory contact between the players and their environment, helps to re-examine and redefine their relationship with that environment.

Jam

One teacher found this variation of *Wading* successful with her first and second grade remedial classes. The children had difficulty imagining the space "changing," so she brought a jar of jam to class and the children looked at it, smelled, tasted, and felt it. She then asked them to imagine that the whole room was filled with the jam and had them walk about in it. Afterward, she asked them to describe their feelings. She repeated the game using milk, fruit juice, sand, and mud. The children enjoyed the game and it helped reinforce their sensory observation and sense memory, as well as the flexibility of their imagination.

Space Adventure

Observers of these games often comment on how realistic and convincing the movement of the players can be, despite their general lack of any formal acting training. It is quite true that were a trained mime artist to prepare a scene of this kind he would analyze the type of illusion he wanted to create and would consciously control the various parts of his body in order to achieve the desired effects. Obviously, this approach is not applicable with amateurs or children. What takes its place is the powerful effect of a strong dramatic image working on the imagination of the player. Thus, if you can really get "inside" the image, you find that your body will react naturally and the results will be quite realistic.

In *Space Adventure*, the director adds all sorts of elements to a changing environment. The players are asked, let us say, to imagine they are strolling in the country on a balmy spring evening. The birds sing in the trees, a faint breeze brings country aromas of flowers, fields, cows, pine trees. There is grass underfoot. Gradually the wind increases in force, the day grows dark, it becomes colder, a few drops of rain are felt on the face. The players seek shelter but none is to be found. The rain dashes down, the wind howls, the players fight against it and are forced onto all fours. The earth trembles and shudders, the ground tilts — chaos has come again! Gradually the earth calms down, the rain stops, the wind drops. The players get to their feet and walk through a thick mist. Soon a star is seen, shining faintly through the mist as it clears, revealing a fine starry night. The moon rises and then, gradually, the scene transforms itself back to the playing area. The players relax, exchange a few words, feel strangely drained. For many it has been a memorable experience.

Sense Diary

This is a valuable written exercise that can later provide material for further creative writing activities. The players are asked to choose a quiet place, such as the corner of a garden, a cellar, a quiet lane or an empty room. They must write down, in as great detail as possible, what they can see, hear, smell and feel. They should confine themselves to actual sensations and leave out emotional comment. This is because emotional, poetic, description tends to edit sensory input. The result is often vague and stereotyped, instead of sharp, closely observed reporting. There is a parallel here to the teaching of drawing. Children usually learn to draw, not what they actually see, but symbols of the world around them, which are recognizable, but don't in fact resemble the object being drawn. The children then become frustrated because their drawings don't look realistic. Requests that the children try to use their eyes and draw what they see are often received with considerable resistance. For further discussion of this problem, I refer the reader to the fascinating and valuable book by Betty Edwards, *Drawing on the Right Side of the Brain.*

It is advisable to choose a quiet place for the first exercise in order to avoid too great a wealth of sensory input that could literally take days to record in all its richness. Later on, when the ability to take in everything has been developed, it is possible to choose other subjects, such as a friend, or the same spot seen at different times of the day. It is also possible to make a conscious choice to omit certain details and to include others. This, however, will not be the result of inadequate observation.

Exercises

• Read your sense diary entry to the group. The other players try to create their own sense of the place. If you do not name the place, they can try to guess where, or what kind of place it is.

UNIT 5:
COORDINATION AND INTERACTION

Through the Thou a person becomes an I.

Martin Buber, *I and Thou*

Introduction

In the following group of games and exercises, the emphasis returns to awareness of others and interaction with them. Most of the activities also aid the development of mental and physical coordination at both individual and group levels.

Mirror

In this well-known game, the players work in pairs, facing each other a step or so apart. Player A initiates a series of simple hand and body movements and Player B becomes a mirror, simultaneously "reflecting" A's movements by copying them as accurately as possible in real time. This requires concentration, coordination and cooperation. Player A should not throw Player B off balance by sudden or jerky gestures, or by moving too fast for B to follow, but should nevertheless seek expressive and varied movements. Eye contact must be maintained, since if, for  example, you turn your back on your mirror, he must turn his back on you and can no longer see what you are doing. Miming specific activities, such as combing the hair, should also be avoided at this stage.

After a time, the players switch roles and thereafter do so with increasing frequency. We try to reach a point when an onlooker is unable to tell who is initiating the movement. Ideally, we should

41

actually reach a stage when neither of the players is really sure, either. Players have often reported that there came a moment when movement was being spontaneously generated in common. The sense of a closely shared experience was beautiful. As we shall see when we come to dramatic games, this is the true secret of improvisational theatre. When no one player "directs" the scene, but all "go with it," allowing the action to develop spontaneously, the results can be breathtaking.

With skeptical students who have not reached this stage of mutual cooperation, I have sometimes played a trick. I ask them to be my mirror. I make a slight movement to start the exercise and then switch roles without telling them, becoming their mirror and utilizing any small, involuntary movements they make. They, of course, continue to believe that they are following me and the result is usually a series of slow, hypnotic movements, which, to their surprise, they learn that they have initiated.

Some teachers have reported considerable success using this game with children who have body image problems. One teacher noted that at first the children found the game funny and strange and couldn't keep it up for laughing. Once the strangeness wore off, however, they managed to achieve "almost total coordination." Their satisfaction, needless to say, was great.

Mirror II

In this variation, we now allow the miming of simple activities, such as washing, combing the hair, brushing the teeth, or applying makeup. These are activities that one would normally perform in front of a mirror, but other actions can be chosen, like unwrapping a candy. It is important for the "mirror" to stay with Player A's actions and not start initiating. The problem is that since an action such as hair brushing is known beforehand, there is a tendency to substitute one's own mime for careful observation of the partner's actions. Therefore, B must not anticipate A's actions or substitute generalized gestures for them. Player B has a further difficultu in that an action, performed with the right hand by Player A needs to be copied in mirror image, that is with the left hand. For his or her part, Player A must perform the activity fully, clearly, and at a reasonable pace. We again try to conceal from an onlooker who is initiating the action. This effort to confound the spectator results in heightened concentration and intense involvement with the problem.

At this point it may also transpire that miming a simple, everyday activity is not as easy as one would imagine. Details of the action suddenly become elusive and players find themselves forced to ask how they actually do light a match, or whatever.

King of the Circle

It is often the case that teachers or group leaders use games with their classes for little other reason than the enjoyment the children have, or the need to fill in a gap in the regular schedule of activities. They are often unaware of the educational or developmental value a tried and true game usually possesses. This well-known game is a case in point. It is excellent for coordination and cooperation, concentration, and observation.

One player leaves the room, while the others sit in a circle on the floor. They choose a group leader who initiates a rhythmic movement using hands, arms, head, body or legs, which the others copy as closely as possible. The first player enters and must guess who the leader is. The movements are changed every half-minute or so. One of the secrets of concealing the leader, of course, is to avoid looking directly at him or her, but at whoever is directly across from you in the circle. The leader can also make it harder by making gradual, rather than abrupt, changes. When the group is really "swinging" it can drive the spotter crazy. I often take a turn as spotter myself, since the desire to "beat the teacher" increases concentration and effort. Leaders should always be encouraged to seek new and inventive movements, rather than repeating the few old tired stereotyped ones. One possible variation has the group moving in a circle, or around the room in a chain, instead of remaining seated.

Follow Me

The players stand in a wide circle and choose a leader who invents a body movement — jumping, skipping, swaying, and using the whole body as unusually as possible. The others copy the movement as fully as they can, as they follow the leader around the circle. After a minute or so, when it is seen that all the players have mastered the movement and coordinated with the others, the leadership passes to the next in line, the previous leader becoming the "tail" of the circle. The new leader allows a new action to grow out of the previous one. The game continues until all have taken a turn at being leader.

Nobody should try to plan the movement he or she is going to initiate. This should arise spontaneously, developing organically from what went before. It may well be quite different from the previous action in form and rhythm, but should result from the new leader following an impulse. This is easier to say than to do, since we are rarely able to allow strict mental control over our actions to relax, or give up our desire to appear "normal," or "graceful," or "dignified." One way to achieve this is not to allow oneself time to think when the leadership is passed to you, but to plunge straight in with an unplanned action. The results are often surprisingly original.

As for the others, they should try to enter deeply into the spirit of the action, trying both to copy the movements accurately and, at the same time, to remain totally free.

Follow Me With Music

In later sections, I shall discuss the value of music as a stimulus for the imagination. In group movement activities, music can, of course, be invaluable in other ways. It provides a steady beat that helps the group coordinate its movements aurally as well as visually, and it provides an emotional framework that helps the generation of spontaneous movement. So, in this version of *Follow Me*, the game is played to the background of a suitable piece of music. The group takes half a minute or so to orient itself to the rhythm of the music, and then the first "leader" takes over. The circle can remain static, or the players can move round the room, as before. The choice of suitable music is wide, but I have found one work particularly successful — "Memphis Underground" by Herbie Mann. Not only does it have an easy but irresistible beat, but it lasts some seven minutes, allowing plenty of time for everyone in a large group to take a turn at leading.

Zig–Zag

The players form two lines facing each other some yards apart. The player at the end of one line makes eye contact with the player opposite, invents a body movement and slowly moves out of line toward the second player. He or she mirrors the movement as closely as possible and also moves forward, till both players meet in the middle. Slowly they circle each other and then move away, still coordinating their movements, till they rejoin the lines (now the opposite line to that in which they started). Player number two now allows a new movement to spring out of what went before, makes eye contact with the next player in the opposite line and the exercise continues, zig-zagging down to the other end. The essential difference between this exercise and *Follow Me*, lies in the powerful effect of the direct eye contact between the players, similar to that in *Mirror*. However, the concentration of the whole group on the developing movement gives the activity its special flavor. This game, too, can be conducted to music.

Unfolding Hands

This game has proved unexpectedly popular with groups of all ages. It not only aids the development of physical and group coordination, but is satisfying in a strangely aesthetic way. Groups of six or seven players form a tight circle facing inward, with arms extended, fists closed and palms upward. One player slowly unfolds the fingers of the right hand, one by one, beginning with the thumb. He continues in the same direction with the fingers of the left hand, beginning, of course, with the little finger and ending with the thumb. Then the player on his left picks up the action, which flows around the circle until all hands are open. The first player now starts closing his or her fingers in the same order and again the action moves around the circle.

We try to achieve a smooth, rhythmic flow of movement around the circle, with no interruptions. It should feel like a rippling wave washing around the circle (similar to the "Mexican Wave" now popular among spectators at sporting events), or as if all the fingers belonged to one giant hand. It helps, by the way, to start with fists tightly closed and to then unfold each finger to its fullest extent. Although a game like this sounds somewhat simplistic, even adults discover difficulties, especially if one aims for a high standard of performance. There is always room for improvement, for at each stage of accomplishment new targets appear. Nobody has yet achieved perfection.

Hands II

Starting with as slow a tempo as possible, we gradually accelerate as we move round the circle, until we are going as fast as we can without sacrificing smoothness or continuity. This can take several rounds of unfolding and refolding. Then we slow down again.

Hands III

Instead of regarding one's hands as a pair, we now make pairs of hands with our neighbors on either side; your left hand with the neighbor's right and so on. This intensifies the sense of sharing.

Hands IV

Now we link arms with our neighbors, so that the two hands in front of us are the left and right hands of the players on either side. As one player commented, "You forget where your own hands are and begin to feel that those in front of you are actually *yours!*"

Hands V

To the physical movement we now add sounds. As each player takes a turn he or she makes a random sound — humming, popping, buzzing, clicking. This sound should be freely associative and can grow out of the previous sounds, or, at least, be a response to them. When we do this with variation *IV*, of course, we make the sound when the two hands in front of us are in action.

Instead of sounds, we can also use words. They can form sentences or, again, be freely associative, springing out on impulse.

Happy Fingers

For children with problems of coordination, the *Hands* game may be too difficult. Here is a simpler version, that also incorporates a color recognition game at the same time.

Take finger stalls in a variety of colors and put them on the children's fingers. Caps made of colored paper, pieces of felt, rings, or the simple marking of the fingers with washable paint, can also be used. The teacher calls out a color and the children raise the finger with that color. The same color can be on the same finger of each child, or on different fingers. Each child can take turns at being leader, raising a finger. The other children identify the color and raise the appropriate finger. They can also work in pairs, pressing together fingers with the same color.

Many developments and variations will spring to mind and the children can be relied upon to make suggestions. Indeed, asking the children to make suggestions should become an integral part of the games process. It becomes a game in itself, and a highly creative one. To give but one example, one child invented a game where the fingers represented children asleep in a big bed. First one child woke up and sat up in bed, then the next child woke up and sat up in bed, and so on.

Hands On — Hands Off

This is another coordination game — the physical equivalent

of a tongue-twister. It is well known. The players stand in a circle and the first player holds out his hand, palm down. The second player places his hand on top of the first, the next player follows suit and so on, till all the players are involved with one hand. The first player now whips his hand away from the bottom and puts it on top, followed by the second, the third — ad infinitum or, at least, till the group breaks up. It's a fun game. A good complication is to include *both* hands, with each player introducing his or her second hand in the second round of the circle. The game has had good success with children who suffer from coordination problems. One teacher started children off individually, each child placing right hand over left, then switching back and forth. Then the children worked in pairs, and finally, in larger groups.

Pinkie!

This is a more difficult version of *Hands On - Hands Off*. Instead of placing hands, palm down on top of each other, each player takes hold of the previous player's pinkie between his or her thumb and first finger. Huge shouts of laughter, groans, mock recrimination and wild applause are heard according to the greater or lesser confusion which develops. The game must be played, of course, at a cracking pace.

Exercises

• There must be plenty of other games involving the kind of interaction and coordination described above. Write down any that you know and present them to the group.

UNIT 6:
COOPERATION

No man is an island.

John Donne

Introduction

The great majority of games and exercises in this book require cooperation between the players. The simple act of playing these games will encourage and develop their ability to cooperate with each other. Here, however, is a sample game that aims specifically at the development of an understanding of the benefits and value of cooperation.

The Card Exchange

Many people, raised in an atmosphere of harsh competition, find it hard to cooperate with one another even when it is of personal advantage to do so. At risk children, in particular, have difficulty "giving up" something, whether it is useful to them or not, or if they are offered something of value in return. This game is designed to accustom such people to relinquish with greater ease in order to gain some advantage as a result. It can help them to understand that "giving in" is not always a sign of weakness, but can lead the individual, or the group of which he is a member, to strength and success.

The game is played with a set of cards with a variety of colors, shapes or symbols on them. Each player receives a set of one each of the different cards. The aim of the game is to exchange cards until each of the players has acquired a complete set of one particular type. Instead of cards, of course, objects such as buttons, paper clips, rubber

49

bands or matches can be used.

This is how *The Card Exchange* is conducted: Each player, in turn, discards one card, laying it face up on the table. Once all have done so, they continue in turn to pick up a card they want and discard a further one, until all the members of the group have achieved their aim of collecting a full set. The process can be timed, to see how fast the game can be completed. Once the game is understood, two teams can compete against each other. Here is a remedial teacher's report of the game, as played in her class of nine difficult boys aged nine to eleven:

In this class the boys demand maximum attention and will do anything to attract it. They are emotionally very immature, quick to quarrel and fight over the slightest matter. They relinquish with great difficulty, finding it hard to give a classmate an eraser, pencil, and so on. Above all, they cannot bear to lose in a game and will fight, cry, and break up the game entirely — anything not to lose.

The children saw me preparing eighty-one cards (nine each of nine different colors) and were very curious to know what was going to happen. I seated them around the table, explained the rules of the game and distributed the cards. The first time around, the boys announced to the group their own chosen color. When I told them to start giving up the cards they didn't need, they fell silent and nobody moved. Eventually they started to grab cards from each other and pandemonium ensued.

The second attempt was also noisy, although this time they were not allowed to grab or demand cards from each other. The third time around, they were not allowed to speak and had to pantomime what they wanted from each other. They did not declare their chosen colors in advance, but had to use their powers of observation. Thus, a problem arose when it became clear that more than one had chosen the same color, but nobody was prepared to be the one to change. This required my special intervention. The fourth time, even pantomime was forbidden and even greater concentration was called for. Finally, they played in teams, competing to see which team could "beat the record."

When the game was first explained the boys didn't want to try it for fear of failure, calling it "complicated" and "childish." It was difficult for them to understand that they had to help the others in order to help themselves. They wanted to collect as many cards as possible, no matter what the color. This desire to get "lots of cards" is a holdover from other popular games in which the one who gets the most is the winner. The alert and more good-natured child who helped his friends was left at the end without a full set and burst into angry tears.

As the children's understanding improved, their enthusiasm grew and so did their sense of individual responsibility for the group's success. They even developed rudimentary strategies for expediting the exchange. Then they got bored by the game's sameness until one of the boys actually suggested shuffling the cards so that nobody knew what cards the others held. This renewed interest, although it also caused renewed conflict.

By watching the boys I was able to observe their individual behavior patterns and to understand them better. They themselves were able to discuss the game later on and to talk about the influence of their behavior on their daily lives.

As an additional activity the group can prepare cards, collect objects and devise variations. Apart from the major objective of helping the children to relinquish, the game helps them to develop sorting and classifying skills.

It should be clear to the reader that many different games and exercises can be devised that have the specific goal of developing cooperative skills. Of course, as you will become aware, cooperation is a main ingredient of virtually all the games described in this book that involve more than one person. Discussion with children will usually elicit from them some understanding that cooperation between people is essential in most areas of life. Examples drawn from team sports like soccer or basketball are particularly useful, since most of the children have some direct experience of them. Those few girls or boys who do not play such sports, usually have cooperative games of their own, like skip rope, that can provide them with the appropriate experience of cooperative activities..

Exercises

• Devise another game that depends on cooperation between the players, using cards or other means.

UNIT 7:
REALITY

Reality...The quality of being true to life; fidelity to nature.

Webster's New World Dictionary

Introduction

Here is a paradox. Our imagination can only flourish when it is firmly rooted in reality. There is a tendency to think of imagination as something fanciful, as an escape from reality, but it should be noted that the *Oxford Dictionary* refers to "the faculty of producing creations consistent with reality." When Wordsworth and Coleridge called it, respectively, "the heightened state of sensibility," and "the sense of novelty and freshness with old and familiar objects," both were implying that imagination is a direct response to reality. It flowers in "...the moment of personal freedom when we are faced with a reality, see it, explore it and act accordingly" (Viola Spolin, *Improvisation for the Theater*). Our problem, however, lies in our actual inability to *see it*, and thus, in our resultant lack of freedom. We are so used to our surroundings that we take them for granted and no longer really look at anything very much. Talking of modern "pop" dancing, a father complained to his son that there was no real contact between partners. "You never look at your partner when you dance with her," he observed. "So what?" replied the son, "I know what she looks like!" Permit me to doubt that.

Most truly imaginative and creative people are acutely aware of the sights, sounds, smells and feelings of the world around them, even if they totally transform it in their work. Picasso can scarcely be described as a naturalistic painter, but his work was based on the most minute observations of the real world. How many of us, for example, have noticed the way a woman turns her head as well as he did?

Dan Cheifetz suggests a possible reason for our generally habitual lack of contact with our surroundings. Cheifetz ran creative play workshops for eight- to eleven-year-olds in New York City, and he noticed that when they pantomimed objects and actions common to their own experience, the objects and actions were mostly vague and generalized. He points out that although

53

babies and toddlers learn mainly by sensory exploration of their environment,

>...now they have reached school age, and their sensory learning is on the wane. For one thing, the repeated dictum "Don't touch" has gotten to them. For another, the important adults in their lives, who used to express their delight with "Watch him push that ball," now pridefully ask their friends to "Listen to him read." In fact, almost all their learning, now a formal rather than a spontaneous process, has become verbal, symbolic and conceptual in nature...with the emphasis so heavy on learning through words and symbols, the information that comes to these children through eyes, fingers, ears, toes and tongue, is unconsciously downgraded or ignored by them. The lack of detail in the children's pantomimes reflected not indifference to the activity and not self-consciousness, but vagueness about real things and actions.
>
> *Theater in My Head*

So here is a series of games that, by requiring us to pantomime actions, makes us focus on what those actions actually involve. By imagining a particular object, we rediscover its reality. When asked whether supplying the children with actual props would not solve the problem, Cheifetz pointed out that, "If they had real props to use, they wouldn't need to pay any attention to them."

Light and Heavy

In this first reality game, the players work simultaneously but separately. This has a double advantage: not only is much time saved but, more importantly, the players get used to the idea that these pantomimes are not primarily for *showing*, but for *doing*. It bears repeating that when actions are pantomimed for an audience, the concentration of the player is often taken up with providing the viewers with clues, rather than with performing the action as fully and accurately as possible.

Each player is asked to imagine an empty bucket or pail standing on the floor in front of him or her. The player must "look" at the bucket and try hard to see it — its size, shape, color and material. The bucket is then picked up by its handle and examined. What weight does it have? What texture? What kind of handle? Does it have a lip for pouring? The player carries it to an imaginary tap (which must also be given reality) and fills it half full of water. The tap is turned off and the bucket carried about the room. How does it now feel? How heavy has it become? The bucket is now "filled" to the brim. How does it feel now? How must it be carried to prevent slopping? Finally, the water is poured out for a suitable, imaginary purpose, such as filling a tank or watering a flower bed.

With younger children, we can do without some of these questions. All we have to do is to get their imagination working, acting out an action with the bucket of water.

As I explained in the exercise called *Space Adventure,* the use of a strong image allows a player untrained in mime to achieve quite remarkable recreations of imaginary objects or situations.

Light and Heavy II

The players work in pairs. Each pair decides on some activity that involves the filling and carrying of some receptacle, works on the action, and then shows it to the rest of the group. Try taking clothes off a line and putting them in a basket, filling a treasure chest, picking oranges, or shoveling sand.

Exercises

- Think of an activity involving a large heavy object and several players.

Fire!

To the above exercises we now add an element of drama. The players are asked to imagine that at one end of the playing area there is a scout shed that they discover to be on fire. The players must form a bucket chain to put the fire out. The first player fills a bucket at a tap, passes it on to the next in line and fills a second bucket. The last player, nearest the fire, receives the first bucket and flings the water at the flames — taking care to direct the water efficiently — runs back to the tap with the empty bucket, fills it and passes it on. This gives each player a turn at filling, passing on and throwing. The group leader provides a running commentary, coaching, describing the state of the fire, and keeping the excitement high. "See the flames!" "Smell the smoke!" "Hurry!" "Don't waste water!" "Look out, the wall's bulging out!" If the players get caught up in the action, a sense of urgency and commitment develops. Afterwards, everyone is exhausted, but happy.

It's Stuck or Something

As I have said, it helps if a game that has the aim of the rediscovery of reality, takes the form of solving a problem in which the player can become involved. In this case, each player is asked to imagine that he or she is having trouble with some small article, such as a tightly knotted shoelace, a worn can opener, a stuck zipper, or a pair of tight boots. The player simply concentrates on overcoming the difficulty. However, the game is not played properly if the player just chooses to solve the problem easily, announcing, let's say, that the zipper came unstuck, without really having experienced the difficulty. This is mere avoidance of the mental effort involved.

When it is taken seriously, the game creates much amusement and provokes sympathetic groans and rueful laughter. One student could not sit by while her friend struggled with the clasp of her "necklace," but was impelled to get up and help her. "I know it's only a game," she explained, "but I couldn't stand it any longer!"

A remedial teacher attending one of my weekly courses reported that her class was much more inventive in suggesting difficulties with objects than the adults in the course. Among others, they suggested and tried out threading a fine needle with coarse thread, and getting a piece of grit in the eye while riding a bicycle.

Let's Skip Rope

Two players pick up an imaginary rope and start to turn it over in the manner traditional to dozens of rope-skipping games. Once they have established the reality of the rope and have found a good rhythm, the other players take turns to "jump in," skip to the rope and "jump out," according to the rules of whatever skipping game has been decided upon. The game involves a number of elements: it's a good physical warm-up, it involves the imaginative creation of reality, and requires good group coordination and concentration.

With a little practice, the rope takes on an astonishing reality and everyone can see at once when a jumper is successful or is "out." I was surprised and delighted that even normally blasé students, never too eager to perform energetic physical exercises, actually requested the game on subsequent occasions. With children, too, it proves a winner. The girls, of course, are eager to show off their skills in a physical activity where, for once, they usually have greater expertise than the boys. It is gratifying to watch how the group can get caught up in the game, with shouted instructions, cries of encouragement or annoyance, remembering the fact that the rope exists only in their collective minds, virtually forgotten. To see a normally disruptive and cynical boy standing by the "rope," rocking backward and forward as he concentrates on getting his timing right before jumping in, is splendid. Afterwards, the players are often tired and enthusiastic, not only at their success, but at the realization that the rope did indeed seem to materialize.

I must sound a word of caution after all this enthusiasm. As always, much depends on the group leader and the preparation of the group itself. No game is a sure-fire winner in and of itself, and if a teacher expects the game to do it all, disappointment will be the inevitable result.

Play Ball

This most basic of all reality games is both simpler and more difficult than *Let's Skip Rope*. The group forms a circle. A player then picks up an imaginary basketball which is thrown from hand to hand. This is very easy as long as the group fulfills one essential requirement. *The ball must have absolute reality.* This, however, is far from easy and needs total concentration, cooperation, and sensitivity. Because an imaginary skipping rope has two ends that are kept in the hands of the two turners who establish a steady rhythm, it is easier to keep in focus, but the "ball" flies through the air and is easy to lose.

So everyone must see and feel the same ball; it must have the same size, and weight (and even color) during the game. All the players must see the same ball in flight and must be convinced that it is truly caught each time. Reality is lost and the ball disappears if the ball that is caught is smaller or bigger than the one that was thrown; if it is thrown weakly, but caught above the head; thrown strongly, but caught effortlessly with no bodily reaction. It cannot divide into two, so if two players each think they have caught it at the same time, someone hasn't really watched the ball and it again disappears. Thus, if players lose sight of the ball they should resist the temptation to fake it and should simply pick up another ball. In any case, it is usually obvious to the others when this happens.

At first, *Ball* causes a good deal of frustration. Instant success cannot be expected. Time and effort are needed and if just one of the players fails to take the game seriously enough, a truly satisfying experience will be denied to all. It is sometimes necessary to bring a real ball, just to remind the players what it feels like, but this should be abandoned as soon as possible. It is also useful to play slow-motion ball. When I performed Theatre Games before an audience we always included a session of *Ball* in our program. When it was going well, the audience was truly amazed at how real the ball became and when we would, without warning, toss it to one of them, the spectator nearly always instinctively caught it, or ducked, to the vast amusement of the others.

With younger children, we start working in pairs, or with the teacher playing with one or two children. It is important to begin with a real ball for a minute or two.

Remember, however, that these games are not simply an end in themselves. They provide an enjoyable framework for the development of valuable and creative personal attributes and lead on to more complex dramatic games. In a sense, *keeping your eye on the ball* is a perfect metaphor for the creation of a group reality whenever a dramatic scene is played. It is in this fact that the importance of *Ball* lies. In a real sense, it is the key to much success in life.

Ball II

When the players begin to master the basic game, balls of different kinds are introduced, like medicine balls, beach balls, or balloons. Balloons are a particular favorite. They can even be changed in midflight, with the recipient instantly changing his physical reactions as the group leader calls out the changes. Now, different objects can be substituted for balls. Try crystal goblets, eggs, or hand grenades. How about a piece of raw liver?!

Ball III

Once players are really good at creating balls and keeping their eyes on them, we can try actual ball games, like Ping-Pong or volleyball. Teams are selected and umpires chosen and regular rules observed. Nets, tables, bats, etc., should have the same reality as the ball and should not alter in size, height or weight.

Tug of War - Preparatory Exercise

Each player imagines a rope hooked firmly to the wall at waist height. He or she picks it up, feels its weight, texture, and thickness, and then pulls on it as hard as possible. The player must try to feel the reality, solidity and thickness of the rope. The advantage of using the wall as the opponent in this preparatory exercise is that it is easy to imagine the wall's resistance. It is equally hard to imagine that we have the strength to stretch or snap the rope.

What actually happens when we oppose an imaginary force in a game of this type and really feel the tightening of the muscles and the strain of pulling, is that we create, by means of a dramatic image, an *isometric tension* between different parts of our body, similar to isometric or biotonic exercises used in physical exercise routines.

Duel

Tug of War is quite a difficult exercise because it is hard to sense the opposing team's will power and strength. I think this is a result of the two teams pulling *away* from each other, with the imaginary rope as the only connecting element. *Duel* overcomes this problem by making the opponent's presence much more immediate and inescapable. *Duel* really fits better in a later section of this book called *Sensitivity and Communication*, where you will find a much more detailed description.

Two players face each other with their hands held behind their backs. They begin to "attack" each other, trying to make the opponent retreat using every means at their command. At no time, however, are they allowed to use their arms or hands, or to make any actual physical contact. The responsibility for not touching is equally shared no matter who is momentarily on the attack or defense. Thus, it is impossible to reject an attack simply by refusing to respond.

Now you can imagine that you are each holding one end of the same heavy stick or a wooden beam, say, three feet long. You must push your opponent back by pushing on the stick.

Tug of War

Now, working in pairs, the players play a tug of war. Each couple must find the reality of the rope between them, a rope of the same weight and thickness for both. It is not made of rubber and cannot stretch. The players must communicate to each other their

strength, will, and resistance. One player cannot "choose" to win by simply moving backward. The partner must genuinely feel that he or she is being beaten.

Once this stage is reached, the players can work in teams. They must now sense the strength and will, not only of the opposition, but of their own team. Groups working well together have commented that they felt as exhausted as if the rope had been real. That is the point. The rope achieved an imaginative reality as a result of the commitment of all the participants. Onlookers can thus find the competition genuinely exciting and urge on one side or the other.

What Am I Doing?

The players take turns choosing a simple activity and act it out in pantomime, trying to make the action as complete as possible. The onlookers must guess what the activity is and must consider if all the parts have been included and completed. Here it is worthwhile reminding the reader of what I emphasized in the introduction to *Trust* exercises: it is vital that onlookers first mention those parts of the pantomime that were successful or complete before referring to missing or incomplete elements. The performers must never be given the feeling that the others are dismissive, or negatively critical of their efforts. This does not mean, however, that omissions or mistakes should be ignored.

Children can also be asked to give a name to each separate action. In one remedial class, for example, a boy pantomimed doing a clothes wash. The class quickly guessed the activity to the satisfaction of all. He then repeated the activity, naming the various steps; separating the clothes, filling the tub, adding the soap powder, and so on. The class then discovered that he had forgotten to rinse out the soap before hanging the wash out to dry on the clothesline.

Here's a report on a version of this game, prepared by a

teacher who played it with both a regular and a remedial class and then compared the results.

I wrote instructions on slips of paper and put them in a hat. The children drew out the instructions. For example:

1. Chew gum and blow a big bubble.
2. Eat a big ice-cream cone which starts to melt.
3. Eat a hamburger.
4. Try to untie a shoelace and fail.
5. Try to thread a needle with coarse thread.
6. Eat the nicest thing you know.
7. Choose a library book from the shelf.

In the regular class, I let the children read the notes for themselves. They quickly understood and found the game a lot of fun. Typical reactions were: "A super game." "I like making movements." " I tried to be funny." "I like playing pantomime." " I felt like I was really doing it."

In the remedial class, I explained the instructions on the notes and in some cases, demonstrated, to give the children confidence to play. They tried hard to amuse each other and win approval. Their movements were heavy and very short in duration. Here, however, are some of their reactions: "What fun!" "I know how to do everything but they don't." "They just don't make me laugh." "Let's play all day long!" "I'm so hungry, I've got to eat right now." (Note the impossibility of postponing satisfaction.) "Mom doesn't give me money for ice cream." "Dad hates me to waste money on ice cream or gum or anything." "Dad gives me money every day not to bother him."

As these comments show, the children brought up the subject of food and friction with their parents. This led to a discussion about their relationship with their parents. All the children poured out their feelings about this, and for most of them, a very painful subject.

It is interesting to note that the teacher here was flexible enough to allow her lesson to totally change its emphasis as a subject important to the children emerged from the game. Her approach is surely sound, for the game always remains a means to greater self-expression and is seldom — if ever — an end in itself.

I'd Like to Be...

This game was devised by a remedial teacher for her class of third to fifth graders. She asked the children to choose a character they would like to be and then pantomime getting dressed up as that character. Next they had to pantomime some of the character's activities. The class had to guess who the character was.

One girl chose to be a queen. She "put on" a long robe and a crown, walked regally across the room and sat down on a throne. This was easy for the class. They had more difficulty with a boy who chose to be a karate expert, because of the simplicity of the dress, but after a few appropriate actions, all was clear. Another boy became a ghost "in order to frighten the bigger kids." One of the girls wanted to be "class queen," but the rest of the children wouldn't accept this. Here again, we see how a game can bring social problems to the surface and by providing opportunities for acting out and discussing them, can help the class deal with them.

Another teacher, hearing about this game, tried it in her own class, but found that the dressing up and pantomiming was not working very well. She therefore devised her own version. The children told the class who or what they would like to be, and the class then had to think of all the advantages and disadvantages of each choice. Some of the choices and the reasons for them can be revealing. One boy of eight declared that he wanted to be a dwarf. He explained that he couldn't be sent to be a soldier in the army and be killed! (This must be seen in the Israeli context of universal conscription. In addition, it turned out that the boy's uncle had been killed in a military action.)

What's Going On?

We now go back to creating an object or performing an activity using mime, with the players working in pairs: folding a blanket, using a two-handled saw, moving a couch, carrying a large birthday cake with lighted candles. The players shouldn't need to give each other verbal clues or instructions like "I've got the corners of the blanket," or "That's the head of the bed over there." Everything should be expressed and communicated through action alone. In the beginning, we often hear comments like "I never realized how complicated such a supposedly simple activity is. There's so much to remember!" or, "I must go home and see what I actually do!"

This demonstrates, as I suggested earlier, how far we fail to experience or participate to the fullest in our own everyday activities. To those who object that we don't *need* to think about such activities, that it is quite okay to perform them automatically, I would answer that any time we divorce mental from physical activity, or allow our actions to become automatic or mindless, we lose some measure of contact with the very processes of life itself. We begin to lose a vital freedom, the freedom to experience every breathing moment. Indeed, we find ourselves relying upon ever stronger stimuli to awaken our interest and participation, rather like drug addicts who require ever greater dosages to achieve their "high."

It is a short step from making a bed automatically to swallowing a hasty breakfast without savor; from perfunctory working with one eye on the clock, to perfunctory lovemaking. Where does one draw the line? And we often become so involved with our memories, satisfactions and regrets of the past, our hopes and fears for the future, that we neglect the here and now. Our life is created from experiences, but we can experience neither the past nor the future. We can only experience the present, the now. We had better make sure we experience it fully.

We all know people who seem to live their lives more fully than the rest of us. Their energy and enthusiasm seem boundless and it is ironical that we sometimes refer to them as "larger than life." Is it not possible that it is we who are smaller than life? Yet this ability to get the most out of life is no mysterious God-given talent. It can be acquired and developed. Yet, as with physical fitness, mental fitness takes exercise. You don't so much learn to be aware, as become, through practice, habituated to awareness.

Exercises

• Think about some activity that you don't like but you have to do. Ask yourself why you don't like it. Now act it out, trying to make the pantomime as full as possible.

All Together Now

Three or more players agree on an object that cannot be handled without involving them all in combined physical activity. Try moving a piano, carrying a heavy box upstairs, erecting a flagpole or a large tent, or pushing a stalled car. This is a logical development from *What's Going On?* and the same comments apply.

It's a good idea here, especially with children, to involve the onlookers by having them suggest the activity. Teachers often comment on the inventiveness and originality that children can display in their choices of activity. One group of eight-year-olds added a nice complication to the problem of carrying a heavy box upstairs by encountering, halfway up, a couple on their way down with bags of garbage that showed signs of bursting any moment. The struggles to squeeze past on the narrow stair were very convincing with lots of authentic detail.

One teacher complained that it was hard to prevent bossy children from ordering the others about. One can partly solve the problem by appointing group leaders, who are changed each time, to direct the action. This encourages the less aggressive children to express themselves and to develop their organizational ability. Later on, the game can be repeated with group leaders specifically prohibited.

Join In

One player is chosen to start an activity without telling the others what it is. When they recognize what he or she is doing, they join in. Instead of a physical object that is to be handled by all, we now have a shared activity. Try sweeping and tidying a room, setting the table, picking fruit in an orchard, or setting up a picnic.

This group interaction should create a dynamic flow and release of energy. Everyone should be busily occupied, paying attention to what the others are doing, neither duplicating effort nor getting in each other's way. Where two or more need to cooperate on some sub-activity, they should not need to be directed; they should simply cooperate in spreading the picnic cloth, carrying away a box full of fruit, or what have you.

Join In II

Readers have probably noticed that a slightly dramatic element is creeping into some of these group activities. The fact is, that whenever a group of players perform some activity together, a simple story line is likely to emerge. As long as we concentrate on making the objects as real as possible and the actions as complete as possible, a feeling of the creation of a satisfying, rounded whole, with a beginning, middle and end, will result. The mistake is to concentrate on the story, while ignoring the reality.

In this version, we take the matter one stage further. Again, one player starts an activity, but this time as a specific character in a specific milieu. When the others identify the character and activity, they join in, performing related activities, also in specific roles. For example, a player enters the playing area. We see her washing and drying her hands meticulously, putting some kind of mask over her mouth and stretching both hands in front of her waggling her fingers. We recognize a surgeon preparing for an operation. A "nurse" runs up to help her put on rubber gloves and smock and then busies herself with the surgical instruments. A patient climbs on the table and is prepared by another nurse and an anesthetist who checks his apparatus. A worried relative paces about outside. We see a dynamic interaction of related actions building up a coherent picture.

The rule here is simple, but it is the rock on which all great acting is based. Don't play *at* the activity, simply *do* it, paying attention to the others as you would in a real life situation. Talk is not forbidden, but should be purposeful and to the point. The object of this game remains the creation of the reality of an operating theatre and not, for example, to show a drama unfolding between nurse, anesthetist, and surgeon. That is a different game that can best be attempted once players have become habituated to creating and maintaining the reality of the physical scene and activity. This does not mean that the characters should have no personality, but merely that the concentration is elsewhere.

On one occasion, for instance, a player, yawning mightily, entered and sat down at what was evidently a huge sack of potatoes and started peeling. Another player entered and said authoritatively, "Leave that just now. Start slicing the bread for the officers' mess." Yes, early morning in an army kitchen was underway.

The Importance of Place

Here are some games that focus our senses on the world around us and help us to recreate various environments in our minds. For at risk children they constitute another link in the chain of activities that can help them to organize everyday experience into a comprehensible matrix of concepts. As with our muscles, our imagination must be exercised for it to develop.

How Do I Know Where I Am?

The teacher or group leader starts a discussion with a group on how we know where we are. The most obvious and simple comments are to be encouraged. "We can see where we are." *What do we see?* "The place." *How do we know what place?* "By the way it looks. By the things that are there." The idea is to focus attention on the things around us which provide us with natural orientation, to think about them and try to visualize them. For children, the effort to describe the difference between various places, or rooms in a house, helps the development of verbal skills and analytical thought. What is the difference between an office and a study? The parents' and the children's bedrooms? A dining hall and a restaurant?

Where Am I?

The players take turns to choose an environment or place. I actually prefer Viola Spolin's term, a *Where*: take a moment to try to visualize it clearly and then enter into it. By actions and manner, the player shows the others where he or she is. If the player has chosen, say, a kitchen, we must "see" the sink, table, cooker, cupboards and refrigerator, while the player performs simple and appropriate actions. The reality of the objects in the room should not vary — the table, for example, can't get higher or lower, or change its position. Nor should the player forget that it exists and walk through it on the way to the refrigerator. The simplest, most common actions, such as opening or closing a door, become mysterious and strangely unfamiliar and need to be reinvestigated.

Gradually, as the players become more confident and skillful, they can be asked to choose a more unusual *Where*, such as a cellar, a public library, a beach, a hospital ward, a bus station, or a prison. Children can be helped by asking them questions that pinpoint the essential elements that define one particular place or another. In one class, for example, a girl went up to an imaginary shelf, mimed pulling out a book and leafing through it. A discussion followed. Was this enough to know where she was? No, it could be her house, a book shop or a library. What was needed to make the place clear? She tried again and this time searched up and down several rows of shelves till she found the book she wanted. Was *this* enough? No, it could still be a book shop or a library. On her third try, before looking for the book, she mimed going up to a cabinet, pulling out a drawer, leafing through an card index, finding the right card, writing down its particulars and closing the drawer. This was certainly a library.

Other questions also arise about the way a person behaves, or is supposed to behave, in a particular place. In your own home you can run, or whistle, or even throw books on the floor (maybe), but in a library one is expected to behave differently. *Why?* "Because you'll get into trouble if you don't." *Why would you get into trouble?* "Because noise disturbs other people in the library who are trying to read." And so on.

Creating an Environment

This exercise helps the group focus on some simple environment and hold it in the memory. One player chooses a *Where*, enters the playing area, handles, in mime, some appropriate object that helps us to recognize the place, and then leaves. A second player must now enter, may relate to the object already created or not, but must create a new object. Then a third player adds something else, and so on. In one class, for example, a player entered, picked up a record, took it out of its sleeve, dusted it off, placed it on a turntable, turned on the stereo, moved in time to the music and left. A second player turned down the volume of the stereo and opened a window. A third player turned off the record altogether, closed the window and sat down at a table to write a letter. Note that since miming sitting down is extremely difficult, not to say uncomfortable, chairs can be used in all these games, but all other props or furniture should be mimed. Occasionally, a table can also be used.

Where Are We?

This is rather like *Join In*, except that here the emphasis is on the place and less on the activity itself. Each player finds something to do that is related to the activities of the other players principally by the location in which they take place.

For instance, a player enters the playing area pushing a shopping cart, examining shelves, consulting a shopping list and putting various items in the cart. This clearly establishes a supermarket. Other players become a check-out girl, a clerk stamping prices on cans, an employee trimming beef at the meat counter and the manager talking on the phone to a supplier.

Once the idea of imaginatively creating an environment has been practiced, the *Where* should automatically be created as a background to any other game involving acting or pantomime. Whenever you see your environment clearly, it becomes much easier to act naturally within it. Your walk, your way of looking, even your breathing and thinking change in accordance with your milieu.

When the great actor, Paul Scofield, was cast as Prospero in *The Tempest* by Shakespeare, I'm told that he prepared for the role by spending a couple of weeks on a small island in the north of Scotland. Then, when he returned to London for rehearsals on stage, he was able to use his sense memory to recreate for himself the sights, sounds and feel of the island, the wind and spray on his face, the pebbles underfoot, and so on. The stage then *became* the island for him. His body language and voice changed and his acting thus gained tremendous conviction and presence.

This ability to observe, absorb and recall a physical reality, was the key which unlocked the wardrobe of his imagination in order to dress Shakespeare's poetry in the fabric of living physical images.

Exercises

• Think of another game that involves handling imaginary objects.

• After playing *Where Am I?*, go to the real place you pantomimed and look at it carefully. If needed, make written notes. Practice moving about the place and handling the objects in it. Note the elements you forgot the first time. Then pantomime the results in the next workshop.

• Teachers can take a group of children to a chosen place and help them perform the above exercise.

• Improvise a short scene between two people. Make sure that the sense of the reality of the place is strong. Now, change the conditions. For instance, if it was a hot day the first time, now imagine the same dialog on a freezing cold day, or when it's pouring rain. Imagine the scene when the two people are quite alone, or when they are in a crowded place where other people can hear them.

SENSITIVITY AND COMMUNICATION

Every person has the need to be touched and recognized by other people.

Muriel James and Dorothy Jongeward, *Born to Win*

Introduction

Communication between individuals is surely the bedrock of civilization. Without it, all would be distrust, fear and aggression, and the life of man would be, in Thomas Hobbes' famous dictum, "solitary, poor, nasty, brutish and short." Yet, many of us live our lives communicating on the most superficial level. As Muriel James and Dorothy Jongeward point out, "People can live and work together for many years but never really 'see' or 'hear' each other."

Part of the problem seems to lie in our egotistic feeling that communication consists of *our* telling *other* people what *we* want or need. True communication, of course, must involve a genuine two-way flow of giving and receiving. This demands the development of the individual's sensitivity toward others.

There's Plenty of Room

Several of the players, or if the workshop is roomy enough, the whole group, begins to walk around the space. After taking a moment to become acclimated, they close their eyes and continue walking. The aim of the game is to continue walking at a reasonable pace without bumping into each other, or into the walls. It thus has an affinity with the *Trust* exercise I call *Solitaire*. At first, much hesitation is felt, with frequent stops and the need to "peek"; people tend to use their hands frequently to fend off walls and each other. Gradually, however, as sensitivity increases and confidence is gained, the players move a little faster and collide with each other less. At the end of each session the players halt. Still with eyes closed, each player tries to sense which of the other players is nearest and where that player is standing. When they think they know, they open their eyes and check. There is great delight when players

69

discover that their inner senses have not betrayed them, and even the skeptics in the group gradually come to realize that the task is not impossible.

Telepathy

In his seminal book on the theatre, *The Empty Space*, Peter Brook describes an acting exercise:

...We set an actor in front of us, asked him to imagine a dramatic situation that did not involve any physical movement, then we all tried to understand what state he was in. Of course, this was impossible, which was the point of the exercise. The next stage was to discover what was the very least he needed before understanding could be reached...

An actor sits at one end of the room, facing the wall. At the other end another actor, looking at the first one's back, not allowed to move, must make the first actor obey him...(using) sounds, for he is allowed no words.

On a never-to-be-forgotten day I was conducting a class of first-year acting students and I incorporated the above exercise in the lesson. I seated two students one behind the other and told the second one to ask the front student to perform some simple action purely by thinking it. I assumed, of course, that he would be unable to do so and that we would then explore the minimum means necessary for communication. Three or four minutes of tense silence followed until suddenly the student in front turned around and stretched her hands out to her classmate sitting behind her. He actually burst into tears because this was precisely what he had wanted her to do! I was as moved and astonished as everyone else present. We immediately repeated the exercise with other members of the group and achieved a significant rate of successful communication. We repeated the exercise at the next lesson and one student became very agitated and broke away, shouting "No! No!" She wasn't sure what she was objecting to, but the second student (who had been absent the first time and misunderstood my instructions) then told us she had been communicating the message "Be ugly!"

Needless to say, this exercise became a regular part of our routine, although I made my view clear to the students that its principal value lay in the extraordinary mutual concentration that resulted and in the powerful sense of shared experience felt by the participants. However, it does demonstrate the potential for communication that lies within us. I have repeated the exercise in various groups with varying degrees of success or failure, and it can be of great value, as long as the players do not set out either with inflated expectations for telepathic communication, or with a contrary sense of cynical rejection. It is probably unsuitable for groups of younger children.

Exercises

• Find another simple situation in which to try telepathic communication. If it doesn't work, go back to adding noises, motions, or whatever else is needed to communicate the ideas.

Don't Come Too Close

Researchers have noted that when people are grouped together they unconsciously tend to seek out a "comfortable" distance from each other. The space that we seem to need between ourselves and others varies widely according to the situation and the norms of a particular society. Thus, in a crowded bus, at a fairground, or family celebration, we can tolerate much closer distances and even full bodily contact. Also, the norms for different societies are not the same. For example, it seems that on the whole Americans tolerate greater proximity than the British.

In this exercise, two or more players enter the playing area and move freely but slowly about in it. Each one tries to find a position which places him or her at the most comfortable distance from the others. Being too far away creates a sense of isolation and being too close creates a sense of oppression. What we may discover is that a comfortable distance for one is not quite right for the other, a constant shifting of position takes place, and a high level of concentration and awareness of each other develops. Aggression, timidity, self-consciousness, or self-confidence find expression in tiny ways, and the exercise can be a fascinating experience. It is unsuitable for most groups of children, however, for whom the purpose of the game is too philosophical.

Exercises

• Try closing your eyes and slowly approaching another player who is standing in the playing area. Sense the presence of the other player and guess how far away you are. Now open your eyes and see how accurate your guess is.

Duel

In the *Reality* section I describe a tug of war played with an imaginary rope. This is quite a difficult exercise because it is hard to sense the opposing team's will power and strength. I think this is a result of the two teams pulling *away* from each other, with the imaginary rope as the only connecting element. *Duel* overcomes this problem by making the opponent's presence much more immediate and inescapable.

Two players face each other with their hands held behind their backs. They begin to "attack" each other, trying to make the opponent retreat using every means at their command. At no time, however, are they allowed to use their arms or hands, or to make any actual physical contact. The responsibility for not touching is equally shared no matter who is momentarily on the attack or defense. Thus it is impossible to reject an attack simply by refusing to respond.

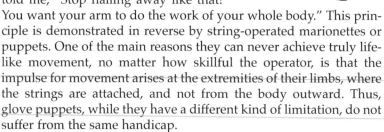

Circling each other, charging, dodging, changing direction, the players seek out their own hidden sources of power, using eyes, head, chest, stomach, hips, legs, and voice. At the same time, they try to find the partner's areas of weakness. Arms and hands are not allowed because we often let them become entirely dominant and their use can prevent us from contacting inner resources. As a tennis coach once told me, "Stop flailing away like that! You want your arm to do the work of your whole body." This principle is demonstrated in reverse by string-operated marionettes or puppets. One of the main reasons they can never achieve truly life-like movement, no matter how skillful the operator, is that the impulse for movement arises at the extremities of their limbs, where the strings are attached, and not from the body outward. Thus, glove puppets, while they have a different kind of limitation, do not suffer from the same handicap.

In *Duel*, strength of will counts for a good deal. I've seen a physically powerful young man reduced to jelly by a fiery young woman half his size. Of course, she was using all the weapons at her command, including her sex, and he just couldn't overcome his chivalrous instincts. I say instincts, but really one could more accurately say that an ingrained social attitude prevented him from releasing his true inner strength. After some discussion and some playful taunting, he allowed himself to get sufficiently worked up to compete with her on more equal terms.

Exercises

- Imagine that you are each holding one end of the same heavy stick of wood, say, three feet long. You must push your opponent back by pushing on the stick.
- Find a string-operated marionette and a glove puppet. Try operating each and see how lifelike you can make simple movements. Compare the two types of movement.

Rhythm Kings

Four ten-year-old school boys are on a bus. The noise is dreadful since, in an effort to hold their attention, each one tries to drown out the others, the phrase most often used being "Hey, Listen!" They — not to mention the other passengers — grow irritated and frustrated. Simply telling them to try listening to each other will have no effect at all.

In our modern competitive society, children learn that "giving in" is a sign of weakness and this attitude often makes even minimal cooperation difficult. I usually ask such children if they have younger siblings. This is frequently the case. I then ask them if they "give in" to their toddler brother or sister who wants a particular toy or something. They usually reply that they do. "Why?" I ask them. "Because he's too young to understand," comes the reply. "Does that mean you're being weak when you let the baby take something from you?" I follow up. "Of course not, it means I'm bigger." In this way I try to bring them to a minimal understanding that giving in can often be seen as a sign of maturity rather than weakness.

Many of the games in this book in general, and in this section in particular, can help children to understand *through doing*, that it pays to listen, that a greater measure of personal satisfaction can be gained by working together than by trying to impose one's own ideas on others against their wills. If you listen to what the other person has to say, he or she is much more likely to listen to you in return.

In *Trust* games, we started building up mutual trust with purely physical exercises as a way of leading up to emotional trust. In a similar way, before we try to achieve this type of mutual sensitivity in conceptual form, for example in dramatic improvisations, we make use of rhythm and abstract sounds.

Rhythm Kings I

Groups of up to seven or eight players sit in a circle. One player starts a rhythmic sound — clapping, beating the floor or making rhythmic sounds with the mouth. The others begin to join in, adding different sounds and rhythms, each player listening hard to the group sound and trying to add a quality or element that seems to be missing. Initial efforts are often tentative and incomplete, or disrupted by a participant who fails to grasp the basic beat. But after a couple of attempts, highly inventive, not to mention "swinging,"sounds often begin to emerge. Once all members are making their contribution to the group sound, the dynamics may alter, getting louder or softer, slower or faster. The players then have a group responsibility for bringing the "opus" to a natural and pleasing conclusion, rather than just stopping in an arbitrary fashion.

One teacher reported that after an initial period of cacophony, her class of seven- and eight-year-olds proved very inventive in the production of different sounds and rhythms. They also came to realize for themselves that, if chaos was to be avoided and a pleasing effect achieved, they simply had to listen to each other. In order to help her class listen even harder, another teacher made them sit in the circle facing outward, so that eye contact was minimal. She reported that concentration was indeed increased.

With young children it is also a good idea to distribute percussive instruments, instead of relying on the sounds the children think of themselves. Later, they can be asked to imitate the sounds of the instruments.

Rhythm Kings II

One player starts, then the others join in, one by one, in order around the circle. When all are participating, the first player, listening to the total group sound, changes his or her contribution to something else. Then the next player does the same, and so on. This produces a continually developing pattern of sound.

As the group becomes more sensitive and experienced, many variations can be introduced. Melody can be allowed or words used for their associative value and quality of sound.

What Did You Say?

This is often used as an exercise to train actors to project their voices without shouting or strain. Basically, however, it is an exercise in mutual concentration and communication. The players form two facing lines. Each pair of players facing each other begins a quiet conversation on any topic of interest. This means that several conversations are being held simultaneously, but nobody is allowed to raise his or her voice in order to be understood. After a minute, both lines are asked to take a step backward away from each other, maintaining the conversations without increasing the volume. Gradually, further steps backward are taken, until the players are as far apart as the room will allow. Then the two lines slowly reconverge. Observers note the extremely high mutual concentration and the careful enunciation that results, and they often comment that it is possible to "tune in" to any one of the conversations and to make out what is being said through the general hubbub. A further complication, added at the end of the exercise, is to have the partners stand back to back and continue the conversation. This is much more difficult and the partners frequently complain of the frustration of not being able to see each other's faces.

Exercises

• Think of another way of needing to concentrate on another player's words or actions. Try your idea out with the group.

Building a Machine

In *Rhythm Kings,* the object is to create a harmonious combination of freely invented sounds and rhythms, with each element contributing to the overall effect. It can succeed only if each player really listens to the contributions of the other players. In *Machine* we add the element of movement. Indeed, movement now becomes the major element in the game. A varying number of players can take part, depending on the size of the playing area and the experience of the players.

Machine I

One player moves into the open space and begins a rhythmic physical movement of a mechanical nature, also making a correspondingly rhythmical mechanical sound. The other players look at him and try to see him as part of an imaginary machine. Each joins in turn, becoming another part of the machine, attempting to add an element that will help to create a whole, a machine that seems to be complete and that operates according to its own inner logic. Once all the players have joined in and the machine is operating, it is the group's responsibility to find a way to bring the round to a natural close, without the need for consultation or outside intervention.

One of the hardest parts of this game is the need to really look and search for what seems to be missing in the machine. All too often, inexperienced players rush in with some superficial or stereotyped contribution that can clearly be seen by onlookers to have no real organic connection with the group work. Sometimes players are embarrassed because they are "taking too long" to find something appropriate. It should be the group leader's responsibility to encourage players to work spontaneously but with feeling. It is better, if one cannot find any contribution that seems right, not to join in that particular round.

The game does call for physical and vocal inventiveness. The players must not content themselves with standing in a vague group making arm movements. A real problem that emerges is the general tendency we have to use the body as a kind of static platform from which the arms operate; players should always look for ways of involving the hips and legs, should look for horizontal parts to the machine, should be prepared to kneel, to squat, or to lie. Great awareness of the other players is needed in order for the sense of an organic whole to emerge.

Occasionally, players have complained that the game is childish. I would rather term it childlike. When taken seriously, with each player's creativity adding to the group effect, participants feel an exhilarating sense of charm, unity and drive.

Machine II

In this variation, an extra player joins in as the machine "operator." Once the group has created the machine, the operator can pull a lever, press a switch, or turn a handle to slow the machine down or speed it up, or to change its mode of operation. No words can be used, but the players must try to feel what the operator is doing and alter their movements accordingly.

Machine III

Here the group leader asks for a machine to be created with specific qualities. Let the machine be powerful, or delicate, fluid, simple or intricate. This is a useful variation since after a few rounds, even imaginary machines can begin to take on a stereotyped quality and creativity wanes.

Machine IV

Up to this point, all the machines in this game have been imaginary. Now we introduce a major change. Instead of an imaginary machine the group tries to recreate an actual one; a sewing machine, typewriter, road roller, computer or washing machine, for example. Some discussion can take place, as long as one of the players doesn't start directing the others. Since it is clearly impossible to reproduce a machine exactly with our bodies, the aim is to create the feel of the machine — its movements, rhythms and sounds.

In one remedial class, the children had some difficulty finding the characteristics of the machines they tried to imitate, but after some practice they succeeded with a cuckoo clock and a typewriter. There was great satisfaction when the rest of the class enjoyed the performance and recognized the machines.

The enjoyment arose from the performance, but note that the game involved the children in *thinking analytically* to break the machines down into their component parts and then to select their most prominent or important ones. Then, however crudely, they had to *synthesize* them into a recognizable whole. This was accomplished by discussion, trial and error, and by working together. This represents a considerable achievement for any group of children, let alone those who are at risk.

Machine V

In this variation, each player, working alone, is asked to produce a machine. The choice of machine can come from the player, the group leader or other players. Several players can show the same item at the same time — we can see five different juice squeezers simultaneously, or the players can take turns. How about a television set, a crane, or a coffee grinder? Remember that the player is free to sit, lie, crouch, or crawl.

Flower Garden

There is a similarity between this game and *Building a Machine*. The players again work together to create a whole, using body movement. Instead of a mechanical object, however, a natural environment, such as a flower garden, is chosen. The players can discuss and choose "roles" such as flowers (single or in clumps), the rising sun, wind, rain, butterflies, bees, and so on. The choices are endless. The players then arrange themselves in the empty playing area.

It is just before dawn. All is still and silent. Slowly the sun rises, lighting and warming the garden. The flowers begin to open, stretching toward the sun. Butterflies and bees flutter and buzz. A light breeze blows, a cloud covers the sun, a shower of rain falls. The sun comes out again and evening approaches. The flowers begin to close, butterflies settle, the sun sets, it is night, and all is silence once more. Perhaps an owl hoots and flits silently by.

This game helps to develop sensitivity, relaxation, liquidity of movement, and tranquillity. One occasion when the game worked well, the players spoke of their "almost mystical sense of communion." Note, however, that a game like this must be taken seriously — one must play the game, not play *at* it. Unlike *Machine*, where giggling or other signs of embarrassment are not particularly destructive, here they can ruin the exercise. The members of the group must therefore be mentally ready to give themselves to the creation of the environment and atmosphere.

Other environments providing good opportunities for group work include underwater scenes such as an aquarium or a coral reef.

One teacher was enthusiastic about the results she obtained with her young first and second grade remedial class:

> Since they were town dwellers with little knowledge of the countryside, I first asked them to look at a giant poster depicting a forest. The children then chose roles, such as trees, birds, animals, and the wind. They then acted out the forest scene, while I played music from *Swan Lake*. I was delighted by the surprisingly effective sense of the countryside that was created, while the children, for their part, were proud and pleased at their success and made comments like, "I really felt cold when the wind blew," "Wasn't I a strong tree?", "I never felt so growing before."

Exercises

• Think of another natural scene to act out. Can you find a suitable piece of music to accompany it?

Living Pictures

Here's a fun game. Each player in turn is allowed to use as many of the other players as necessary to build a living picture — *a tableau vivant* that tells a story. The creator places the characters in the playing area, shows them the gestures and expressions required, and chooses a title. Once all is prepared those not involved guess what the situation is. For instance, one student placed one figure looking up and pointing. A second figure followed his gaze while a third was crouched down behind the second extracting his wallet from his hip pocket. The title? "Criminal Cooperation."

The game gives an excellent opportunity to children who have difficulty competing with their more confident class members. They too can create a living picture to express their ideas — one small step in the confidence building process.

What's Happening Now?

This game can be introduced in two stages, depending on the sensitivity of the group. Some children may find the second stage too difficult, but teachers can devise easier variations.

Variation I — The group splits up into sub-groups of three to five players. Each sub-group takes a turn to move freely around the playing area, running, skipping, jumping, kneeling, crawling, or rolling about. Suddenly, the teacher calls out "freeze" and the players stop in their tracks and try to hold whatever physical position they are in. The onlookers now try to imagine what kind of "living picture" has been set up, as in the game described above. This time, however, no one has planned it, and there is no single right answer. It is important for the group leader to try to find an appropriate moment to freeze the action when the group is in an interesting configuration. The onlookers can then tell the group what living picture they imagined.

Variation II — As in *Variation I*, the group freezes on command. But now the players take a moment to look around and try to sense what is happening, or what is about to happen. In what living picture do they find themselves? They can now unfreeze and improvise a scene of which the living picture is a starting point. This requires great mutual sensitivity between players who must be ready to pick up and recognize the dynamics and the tensions suggested by the physical grouping of the freeze. This variation is probably more suited to those players who have already had some experience of improvising short scenes.

Use Your Whole Body

Here, the players have to find an activity that involves the use of the whole body. This may be quite a realistic scene involving, for example, shifting a car that is stuck in the mud, or erecting a tent in a high wind.

On the other hand, the exercise can be expressionist, abstract, and evocative. For instance, I place a chair in the center of the room and the players spread out around it and are given the following image: an overwhelming impulse drives them to reach the chair and touch it, but the chair emits a terrible force of repulsion. This exercise can have the most powerful emotional effect on players and spectators alike, as the players struggle to reach their goal.

Sometimes a scene can be devised which involves a conflict of character. On one memorable occasion, two students played a scene in which a deep-sea diver, seeking treasure, encountered a mermaid. In slow mesmeric motion they met, showed fear, fascination, and even love. But the greed for treasure was too strong for the diver, who struggled to gather up the precious stones littering the sunken wreck. Picking up a sharp seashell, the mermaid cut his air line and fondled him lovingly as he drowned. The players, in this case, were acting students who had gained an advanced degree of improvisatory skill, and the entire scene was improvised without preplanning. However, even inexperienced or young players can achieve sensitive and imaginative scenes if they have the freedom that mutual trust can inspire.

Gobbledygook

The most immutable barrier in nature is between one man's thoughts and another's.

William James

I do not believe...that the purpose of language is to conceal thought, for I believe that its purpose is to assist and confirm people in refraining from action.

Kierkegaard

If only everyone talked the way we do in my household. I mean...if everyone...like...talked...you know...the way we do...right? It would be so much...like...like...easier...you know...understand...right?

Robert Nordell

Since language is the pre-eminent medium of learning and communication emphasized by our society, one could expect that most people would have a highly developed ability to express themselves in words. But a great deal of effort and positive motivation is actually needed to develop personal language skills. Just as many immigrants to a new country learn just enough of the language to get by, so huge numbers of children make do with a limited vocabulary. Unable to formulate thoughts with precision or express themselves richly or even adequately, they rely on expletives and become easily frustrated, argumentative and rigid. In this context, the book *Lost for Words — Language and Educational Failure* by J. W. Patrick Creber makes chilling reading.

We cannot express what we feel and we do not feel what we are saying. Strangers to ourselves, we soon don't even know *what* we feel. We only know what we are *supposed* to feel in a given situation. Propagandists, advertisers, and politicians, are well aware of this, and by manipulating language create in us the responses they wish us to have. Words, instead of communicating reality, have become a way of masking reality.

The enrichment of our vocabulary should therefore be a major task of educators. But we must first rediscover our inner responses in order to counteract the corruption of our thought. We must learn to feel as we speak and to sense others as they talk to us. To this end *Gobbledygook* is a valuable tool. Viola Spolin (who calls it Gibberish) points out that:

> …Gibberish develops the expressive physical language vital to (stage) life by removing the dependency on words alone to express meaning. Because gibberish uses the sounds of language minus the symbols (words) this puts the problem of communication on a direct-experiential level. The player showing the most resistance to gibberish is usually the person who relies almost completely on words in place of experiencing, and shows great anxiety when words are taken away from him…his everyday body movements are stiff, and his isolation from his fellow players is quite pronounced.

> One anxiety-ridden student who finally received great insight remarked, "You are on your own when you speak gibberish…When you use words, people know what you are saying. *So you don't have to do anything*" (my emphasis).

> Gibberish forces the player to show and not tell. Body holds are released for players must listen and watch each other closely if they are to understand one another.

Although Spolin is speaking primarily about the theatre, what she says is clearly applicable to creative play as well.

What's That?

In this preliminary exercise, I simply ask the players to open their lips and let random sounds come out of their mouths to form nonsense words and sentences. However, to convey this request I speak in gobbledygook myself. Met with initial incomprehension, I persist, using all the expressive means at my command to indicate what I want the players to do. Eventually, they catch on and I then ask them, still in gobbledygook, to turn to each other and hold short babbling conversations. Although actual ideas are not likely to be conveyed at this stage, much animation and hilarious laughter usually spread through the group.

I now convey the idea that the players should ask each other to perform simple tasks — stand up, sit down, open the door, light a match. It becomes clear that the sound on its own is usually inadequate and must be integrated with physical expression and tone of voice. Some players find great difficulty in forming nonsense words and may even show some resistance, often asking "What's the point?"

At this point, I revert to normal language and provide a brief explanation.

Salesperson

Players take turns trying to sell some item in gobbledygook. It must be made clear to the others what is being offered, its advantages, what a good bargain it is, and so on. It is important that the seller work directly with the other players and not address some fictional audience "out there." When the seller is energetic and persuasive some of the other players usually join in spontaneously, acting as prospective buyers, criticizing the product, and arguing about the price. On the other hand, I do recall one student who did a splendid job as a very superior saleslady in a boutique, who demonstrated her gowns with great restraint and even disdain for her clients. Very effective!

Exercises

- Think of another situation in which one person must communicate to others, or an audience. Try it out in gobbledygook.
- Think of a group scene in which everybody can take part, for example, a street market. Try it out in gobbledygook.

That Is Interesting!

Two players start a conversation in their normal language on any topic that interests them. After a minute or two the teacher calls out "Gobbledygook" and in midsentence they must switch into gibberish while continuing their conversation and train of thought. It is important that the players know exactly what they are trying to say, and do their utmost to convey this to their partner, who will have to reply and must therefore understand the gist of what has been said.

After another half minute or so, the teacher calls out "English" (or whatever language is the norm) and the players switch back, again in midsentence. It will be immediately evident to the onlookers if the players have indeed played the game or if they have more or less marked time, making random sounds but not really continuing the train of thought. The game continues with the teacher switching the language back and forth with increasing frequency. This is an art in itself, requiring a high degree of concentration from the teacher.

As long as both players are on their toes, the game can be extremely entertaining. It is delightful to see a player passionately declare "Raba dooli swami pota but he *insisted!*" Especially when everyone knows *exactly what ki leeno!*

As I Was Saying

Two players decide on, or are given, a situation to act out, such as a couple who is late for an important dinner preparing to go out. The whole situation can be played out in gobbledygook or can switch back and forth as above.

All the actions should be as natural and unforced as possible. The aim of the game remains the communication of ideas and mood without over-reliance on words, rather than the development of a highly dramatic or comic situation. I do not mean that the scene should be dull; the players should allow it to develop in any direction that it seems to want to take. As I have already noted more than once in this book, the emphasis should be on doing what needs to be done, rather than actively deciding on dramatic or comic actions. The most effective moments in any improvisation are those arising naturally in context, with one player making some impulsive, unforced, comment or action in reaction to what has gone before. There is nothing less funny than trying consciously for laughs.

During one workshop I performed a scene in which I was the

victim of a traffic accident seeking medical attention at a hospital. My fellow player was the receiving clerk, anxious to help but confused by a new computer system. Both of us concentrated on solving our specific problems and the results, I am told, were hilarious. The following week we tried to repeat the scene — it was a disaster! We were so involved in trying to be funny and trying to remember the good bits from the previous week that the whole thing was a wretched and embarrassing bore.

Nursery Rhymes

For those who continue to have difficulty in speaking gobbledygook fluently, this variation is useful and can be great fun. It is particularly successful with children.

We substitute the words of any well-known nursery rhyme for the gibberish, but apply them in a context quite divorced from their original meaning, using them in any of the variations described above.

One dramatic situation that is a sure-fire hit involves a teenager coming home and finding her younger sister messing with her makeup for the umpteenth time. She has also "borrowed" her last pair of pantyhose! It is notable that whatever nursery rhymes are chosen by the players, their actual words seem to take on real significance, as if they have been chosen deliberately to fit that particular situation.

Another situation, suggested by a teacher in one of my workshops, has a teacher retell a funny story she has just heard about the school principal to the other teachers. These examples suggest that situations taken out of the general life experience of the players are most likely to succeed.

In all these games, the more we concentrate on enjoying the sheer sound we are making, the more we try to make our gobbledygook expressive of our emotions, the more open and responsive does our imagination become.

Exercises

- Think of other situations suitable for gobbledygook or nursery rhyme scenes between two or three people.

- Replay a situation, but switch the two players so that now they are playing the opposite role.

- Replay a situation, but add predetermined mental states to the characters. For example, they can be timid, aggressive, worried about something, relaxed, etc. See how this alters the scene.

Knockity-Knock

This game was devised by a remedial teacher. Two children choose roles and decide on a reason to have an argument. They then sit at a table and conduct the argument using physical expressions and banging on the table with the ends of pencils or rulers, but using no words. The rest of the class has to guess what the argument is about. For instance, two of her pupils chose a mother arguing with her daughter, who had come home late from school and didn't want to tell her where she had been. At first, the class had difficulty, only guessing that the daughter had been naughty, but soon picked up other clues (the mother pointing to her watch, etc.) and came closer to the answer.

The situation was then repeated incorporating speech. After the argument, the characters had to "make up," first using physical means and then using real words.

The game gave rise to a valuable discussion in class. What is the relationship between one's emotional reaction and its cause? Let us say that your little brother plays with a special toy of yours without permission. You get angry. Suppose he breaks it. You get angrier. You scream and shout and hit him. Now suppose that a big bully attacks him in the school yard, breaks his glasses and makes him cry. Shouldn't you be still angrier? But if you already shouted and screamed and hit when he broke your toy, how can you show the difference? What is more important? Maybe you overreacted to your brother. Do we tend to react too violently to relatively unimportant matters, and then have no adequate ways of expressing ourselves when something really important occurs?

The teacher then applied the same principle to the vocabulary we use. In her report to me, she noted:

> If we use big important words to describe something small — an *incredible* pop song, a *fabulous* ice cream — we don't make the song or the ice cream any grander, we just make the words "incredible" and "fabulous" sound feebler. If you always use words like wonderful or gorgeous to describe your latest tee shirt, what can you say about the new baby in the house that you love, the first person landing on

Mars, or real peace between nations? How can you let people know how deeply you may feel about these things? How can people tell that you think them more important than a tee shirt?

She reported that she was then able to conduct a series of lessons on appropriate language that helped to enlarge the children's vocabulary and make them more sensitive to the use of words. One of the children even volunteered the idea that it was best not just to tell people that you love them, but to show them by doing caring things.

Caring Puppets

Finally, let me mention a project run by a friend, Dr. Simon Lichman, in Jerusalem, designed to bring together Jewish and Arab fifth and sixth graders, to learn about each other, and to break down some of the cultural and ethnic barriers between them. A major activity involves the making of simple puppets by the children. These are constructed from sticks, scraps of fabric, buttons, glue, stuffing, and anything else that can be pressed into service. Here is part of a report on the project by Ruth Mason.

...Once the dolls are made, the children are divided into mixed groups of four or five. The task: to come up with a puppet show using the dolls. The kids plunge right in. They use the few words of each other's language they know, a bit of English and much sign and body language to get their plays rolling.

...One group of boys put on a simple meeting-and-greeting play but with their identities changed. The Jews become the Arabs and the Arabs the Jews. A group of girls pretend they are customers and waitresses in a restaurant struggling to understand each other. One group of boys put on a bilingual Little Red Riding Hood. Everybody roars with laughter when Little Red Riding Hood is greeted by the wolf with "Salaam Aleikum."

"The dolls help overcome shyness," says one of the mothers. "You can't create something deep in one or two meetings, but there is an atmosphere of wanting to break down barriers. They get to know each other because they are doing things together. It's the most natural way to make contact."

While the importance of this project is obvious in the strife-torn Middle East, it can just as obviously be applied to groups of children from differing ethnic or cultural backgrounds. Sadly, misunderstanding and prejudice are all too prevalent in modern society.

The use of such puppets can also be incorporated into many of the other dramatic and storytelling games and exercises found elsewhere in this book.

Exercises

• Choose a time to observe other people — in the street, at home, at school, in the shopping mall, etc. — and note how they react to each other. How well do they seem to communicate with each other, and how sensitive are they of each other's needs and feelings? Make written notes, then devise scenes in the workshop to act out some of the observed situations.

• Devise further games involving the use of appropriate adjectives and actions.

When I am in my ship, I see
The other ships go sailing by.
A sailor leans and calls to me
As his tall ship goes sailing by.
Across the sea he leans to me,
Above the wind I hear him cry:
"Is this the way to Round-the-World?"
He calls as he goes by.

A. A. Milne, When We Were Very Young

UNIT 9:
TRANSFORMATION, DISCOVERY AND SPONTANEITY

Through spontaneity we are transformed into ourselves.

Viola Spolin, Improvisation for the Theater

Introduction

The above verse by A. A. Milne and its lovely illustration by E. H. Shepard capture perfectly the child's complete absorption in his game, and his ability to see, hear and feel the world he is creating, while knowing perfectly well that the proud galleon is only a chair.

The next minute it may well become a racing car, house, or store, and a whole new world will be summoned up in which his adventures can continue. Because the child sees this imaginary world so clearly, adventures in it develop naturally and creatively. For most of us, however, this magical eye becomes dulled with time as the "real" world encroaches upon us. Also, there are many at risk children in whom the ability to create an imaginary world never properly develops. Indeed, although advantaged children often have more toys and of a greater variety, they are less dependent on them in their play, replacing them with substitute objects when they are unavailable, or even with purely imaginary ones. "I'm the school bus driver," calls a little girl, vigorously turning a Frisbee that she has transformed for the moment into a steering wheel. At risk children, on the other hand, are more dependent on toys, because their ability to make believe is stunted. Yet this ability to make discoveries by transformation of objects, images and ideas, is an essential part of self-actualization.

There are three complementary types of thought processes that we need to develop to achieve self-actualization. As Richard de Mille notes, the first, called *convergent production,* largely involves the recall of facts and the calculation of right answers, and is certainly of great importance in our daily lives. The second, which invokes a *quantity* or *variety* of appropriate ideas is *divergent production.* This type of thinking is an essential element in all creative work and is intimately connected with the transformational ability I have spoken of above. The third, involving the exercise of judgment through the conscious choice between alternatives, is *evaluation.* Both the latter types are inadequately taught in most school systems, because emphasis is placed on telling, giving facts, and accepting right answers only. Thus, little time is devoted to encouraging pupils to reach their own decisions.

This section describes a number of games and exercises which can help us develop our capacity for divergent production and for spontaneous generation of images and ideas.

It's a Bird, It's a Plane, It's a Superdraw!

For this game we need a blackboard and chalk. When played at home, one of those "magic drawing" pads is useful, or sheets of scrap paper can be used. A simple shape, made up of a couple of lines, is drawn on the board, and the group is asked to see it as the start of a picture of...what? As ideas come to them, the players approach the board and sketch them in. As each image is recognized by the group, it is erased and another player is called up. When invention begins to peter out, a new shape is substituted. Sometimes a major problem is that invention shows no sign of flagging — I have found one shape kept a group of twelve-year-olds occupied for a whole hour, and have had to copy the shape twice more on the blackboard, so that three children could work simultaneously.

One reason for the game's success is the realization — by even the most insecure child — that here is a kind of question to which there is no wrong answer. Even those who are afraid that they will "draw it wrong" are encouraged, when they see that an ability to draw well is unimportant, as long as the idea is recognizable. It is also possible for such a child to make a suggestion for the teacher to draw — the idea remains the child's.

Some teachers have questioned the fact that each idea is immediately erased. Why, they ask, can't we give each child a sheet of paper so that the drawings can be kept after the game? I would say that we can, of course, play the game that way. However, it then becomes less of a shared experience and I also find that the large scale of the blackboard allows the children a greater ease of expression. In addition, too much importance is often attached to the existence of a physical object that can be "saved" after the game is over. It is important we all understand that once an idea has been shared, it no longer needs to be saved on paper — it exists in our heads. Indeed, after the game has been played, we can play a supplementary memory game, in which the players try to remember as many as possible of the various ideas that were produced.

Below I show a couple of typical shapes, and some of the ideas they can generate.

Illustration 14

91

Note the drawing of the house with the setting sun, which was the idea of one ten-year-old. It is of particular interest because the boy was able to see the two component lines as belonging to two different objects making up a single image. Once this concept has been introduced, a huge range of further ideas can be released from the participants' imaginations.

I have recently been working with a blind girl. I tried the game with her, drawing the shapes on a wax tablet for her to feel with her fingers. It was not very successful, however, because her ability to visualize two-dimensional images is not very developed. I then tried using three dimensional objects made out of wood, hardened play dough and so on. This has been more successful, although we still have to do more work on developing suitable base shapes and varieties of material.

Exercises

• Experiment with other simple line combinations, straight with curved, all straight lines, etc.

• Look at real objects and isolate parts of their outlines. Copy these down and try them on the group. See how many different objects can be summoned up, and how many of the players actually envision the original object.

The Bag of Tricks

Over the years, I've built up a useful accessory — my "bag of tricks." This is simply a strong shopping bag filled with a variety of simple, everyday and fun objects. They include a reel of cotton, an electric plug, a box of crayons, a small screwdriver, a dog's leash, a battery, a small plastic bottle, an eraser, a hairbrush, and a plastic clothespin. The choice is infinite as long as the items are familiar and have a wide range of shapes, textures and materials. You never know when the bag will come in handy and there are, of course, specific games to be played with it, such as the following one.

It's Something Else

I spill all the items out on the floor, and invite each player to pick one of them up, and by playing with it to transform it into something else. Once the ice is broken the ideas come pouring out. The box of crayons, with its window to show the crayons, becomes a transistor radio, a pocket calculator, a box of pocket tools. The leash is suddenly a snake, a fishing line, a whip. The screwdriver is transformed into a hand-held microphone, a paint brush, a lollipop. Even at risk children find this activity relatively easy and non-threatening, and thus enjoyable. I recall one bashful nine-year-old hanging back while the others scrambled for the objects. At last she picked up a hitherto neglected clothespin — the kind with a metal spring — and shyly showed us a baby crocodile opening and closing its jaws. For a brief instant it had a lovely reality and the reactions of her classmates were genuinely appreciative (Wow! Great!). Her happy smile was a joy to behold.

Exercises

• Make your own "bag of tricks."

• Look at larger objects. See how they can be transformed in the imagination into something else. In this connection, the television program of theatre games, "Whose Line Is It Anyway?," which became very popular in Britain and the USA, used this idea for one of its most amusing games. Two players were handed some large object, and asked to use it in a variety of imaginative ways. The results were often hilarious. Bring such large (lightweight) objects to the workshop and try them out.

Find the Link

This game requires the preparation of a deck of picture cards. I made mine by looking through a pile of old magazines of different types and cutting out pictures, or sections of pictures, roughly the size of a normal deck of cards. The pictures covered a wide range of objects — scenes, photographs, line drawings, and graphics. They were in color and monochrome, and I added some extra items from my computer printer, my daughter's sticker collection, and a couple of my own hand drawings. The pictures were then glued onto stiff cards, and the whole thing took me no longer than a few hours one weekend. An advantage lies in the fact that one can always add new items and the loss of one or two cards does not ruin the deck.

The object of the game is to find connections between cards drawn at random, or laid out face up on the table. As we play the game, we discover more and more types of links — subject, colors, shapes, uses, living creatures, abstract designs — the possibilities are very wide indeed. Each player takes a turn to select or receive two cards and find a connection between them. The player can find more than one connection. Then the other players have a chance to point out other connections that can be found.

Exercises

- Collect a number of suitable pictures to bring to the workshop. The production of the deck of cards can then be a group effort.

- Make up a collection of physical items with which the game can be played, or use the contents of the room in which the workshop is taking place.

Rummy

This version of the card game *Rummy* was invented by my (then) nine-year-old daughter. It is for two or more players. Like standard Rummy, cards are dealt out, picked up and groups of cards linked by suit, value etc., laid down in turn, until one player has no cards left in his or her hand. In this version, instead of cards being linked by suit, value, etc., groups of cards can be laid down only if they have a common link. Since the discovery of links depends on the ingenuity of the players and their divergent production abilities, it makes for an extremely entertaining game.

Memory Links

Another version is a form of the well-known Memory game in which the cards are laid out face down, and players take turns to try to find two linked cards, using their memory of those cards previously revealed. In its easiest form, suited to younger players, the player turns up two cards and then calls out the linkage between them. In the more difficult form, the player must first declare the link before upturning the cards.

Exercises

- Devise further uses for the deck of cards.

I Went on Holiday and Took...

This game I learned from a student teacher who had played it as a child. A player thinks of a particular link between different objects. The link might be a color, a shape, a use, or a category. Then the player says to the rest of the group, "I went on holiday and I took with me an xxxxx," naming one of the objects. The others think of what might be a matching object and say, "Can I come with you with a yyyyy?" If that object conforms to the link the first player thought of, he or she says, "Yes, you can come with me," but if it doesn't, the reply is, "No, you can't come with me." By listening to the replies of what conforms and what doesn't, the group must guess the link between the objects.

For instance, suppose Player A says, "I went on holiday and took with me a lemon," the others might suggest "an apple" — no; "a buttercup" — yes; "an egg" — no; "lentils" — no; "a Beatles submarine" — yes. By now, most of the group will have guessed that the link is the color yellow, and not the shape, the letter "L" or something that can be eaten.

Here's another example. Player A says, "I went on holiday and took a camera." The others suggest "a transistor radio" — no; "a diary" — yes: "a paperback book" — no: "a sketch pad" — yes. Can you now guess the link?

This game can obviously be played at varying levels of sophistication and complexity. With younger children, the objects can be simple and links can be obvious, while, as the groups become older, they will rapidly start thinking of subtler connections.

A Long Piece of String

Here's a useful item: five yards or so of string or light rope. I actually prefer the kind of lead-weighted cord used to keep curtains hanging neatly, since it has greater stability. It can be used for a variety of activities, such as this one, suggested by an elementary school teacher after successful use in her classes.

How Many Ways?

The cord is thrown down on the floor to form a random line. The players, one by one, must move along it from one end to another, each player finding a different way of doing so — hopping, shuffling, crawling forward, backward and sideways — an amazing variety of methods can appear. The game develops divergent thinking and physical coordination, and is useful for children with certain types of physical disability.

Math, Geography, Etc.

A prop like this can be adapted to lessons in various subjects, adding a spice of novelty to a possibly dry topic. Two suggestions I received were in the areas of elementary geometry and more advanced geography. The mathematics teacher proposed making squares, oblongs, triangles, etc. from the cord, measuring the sides, the angles, the volume and so on. The geography teacher laid the cord out to represent the course of a river. The pupils were required to describe the geographical features of the countryside which might result in such a course. Other questions also arose, like where along the river a town might be expected to develop.

Exercises

• With these examples to provide the spur, think of other entertaining applications for the long piece of string.

Figure-It

Again, we need a blackboard and chalk. The game is based on a simple technique for creating schematic, but very expressive, figures from two lines and an oval head shape. If you try, you will see that almost any combination of two freely drawn lines and a suitably placed oval will create such a figure, as in the examples shown below. I have actually produced well over a hundred such figures mounted on large cards, and have turned them into a prototype boxed game.

Illustration 15

The basis of the game consists of drawing two such figures on the board, surrounding them with a frame, and asking the players to explain who the characters in the picture are, and what their relationship is to each other. In short, what's happening in the picture? The players can simply describe the situation, or can elaborate it into a little story. As in other transformation exercises, it quickly becomes evident that there are infinite possibilities. The figures are sufficiently abstract to be interpreted in various ways: can be looking ahead, to the side or backward, can be male or female, younger or older. Illustration #16 on page 97 shows how small changes can alter the effect of what is essentially the same figure.

Illustration 16

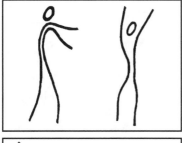

1. "Hands Up!"
2. "Is It Really You?"
3. "You're Outta Here!"
4. "Defense! Defense!"

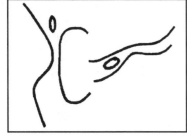

1. "Help! Murder!"
2. The Winner of the Race
3. The Circus
4. The Skiers

Illustration 17

Variation I — Titles

In this variation, the players must think of a short title that makes the action clear. This also involves development of language skills, requiring the player to concentrate on the essential element in the action. Above are two such drawings reconstructed from a session with twelve- and thirteen-year-olds, with just a few of the titles they came up with.

Variation II — Fill in the Background

Not everyone has the same level of verbal skill and some children may be considered dull when actually they are simply more visually oriented. Here the players make their ideas clear by drawing an appropriate background, as in the following examples:

Illustration 18

Variation III — Act It Out

This time, the players work in pairs and act out a short scene based on the picture. It may be little more than a living tableau, or can be elaborately developed. The attitudes of the characters in the picture can appear at the beginning, in the middle, or at the climax of the scene. Here, many additional playing skills can be developed, of course, and this version of the game could be logically included in many of the sections of this book, such as those dealing with cooperation, spontaneity, and dramatic improvisation.

In one such session, with ten-year-old at risk kids, I used the combination of the kneeling and standing figures shown above. Two girls worked together and asked me to include a third girl (a particular friend). This was their scene. A harassed mother gives her unwilling daughter money to run to the grocery store to buy bread. After an argument, she agrees, but meets her friend on the way and they stop off to play hopscotch. When the girl eventually goes to the store the money is gone — it must have fallen out of her pocket while she was playing! With her friend, she runs back and searches the ground on her hands and knees while the friend looks around. The money is found and, thankfully, she completes her errand and goes home to her now worried mother. This simple episode, based so naturally on the immediate lives of the young players, gave them and the whole group a great deal of pleasure and satisfaction. The girl who played the mother had a great time and obviously used language and figures of speech she had heard from her own mother under similar circumstances.

Surprise Yourself

In the section on reality games and exercises, I introduced the idea of creating an imaginary object and endowing it with a sense of physical reality. In this exercise we take this idea a step further.

Each player is asked to reach out with his or her hands and try to let them encounter an imaginary object. Once the object has been discovered it should be felt, examined and, if possible, used. As far as possible, the object should come as a surprise to the player, who should not decide in advance what object is to be "found," but should allow his or her hands to find it, even if this takes some time.

Having fully experienced the object, the player then allows it to transform into something else. (As I was typing this, I stopped and tried the game again for myself. Reaching into space I "encountered" a ball of cotton. I fingered it, touched it to my face, breathed through it and then, as I began to tear off a piece, I found myself tearing a check out of a checkbook instead. I accepted the transformation and carried on with the new action. In no way was this planned consciously.)

Why *not* consciously? On a simplistic level, because that's a different game. However, a more important reason is that by allowing the transformation to take us by surprise, we are reaching for a subconscious impulse, a free association of ideas, and thereby increasing the possibilities for creativity and the fascination of the game. As in other games (notably, in *Finger Theatre*), players can become enthralled, waiting to see what will happen next.

Pass It On

The players stand in a circle facing in. One player "finds" an object, handles and uses it, and passes it on to the next player. This player accepts it, and also handles it until it transforms into something else, handles and uses the new object and passes it on. The object must be given sufficient reality for the other players to see it clearly, and this need gives rise to great concentration. The whole group finds itself concentrating equally hard to discover what the object is. However, even if the recipient is not sure what object he or she has been given, all that is needed is to let some object be discovered, and the game can continue. Of course, the greater the reality of the objects, and the more unexpected the transformations, the greater will be the enjoyment of all concerned.

On one occasion, a girl student in one of my acting classes was handed a "chest expander" by the previous player. When she tried to expand it, the springs were "too strong" for her, and sprang out of her grasp. As her hand absorbed the recoil, she started, her eyes aglow. On the back of her hand she could see a number of precious stones, which had sufficient reality for the rest of us to sense something special, even before she picked them up and played with them. That was a moment of perfect transformation.

Sculpture Garden

As I have already demonstrated in *The Amazing Classroom*, we tend to ignore much of the world around us. As we become more "mature," our eyes become jaded and our imaginative, transformative powers become rusty. Here is an activity that can help us see familiar objects with a fresh eye.

Each player picks up a chair and examines it, feeling its textures, handling it, holding it up, perceiving its lines — even smelling it. Does it have a personality? If it were a person, what kind of person would it be?

Working in pairs, the players now try to form a sculpture from their two chairs, discovering the variety of ways in which two chairs can be grouped together. In the beginning, people sometimes say "how can you make anything interesting out of a couple of chairs?" After a few minutes of trial and error, however, it becomes apparent that the possibilities are many. When several "sculptures" are ready, the players walk around the "exhibition" admiring each other's work. The results can be truly imaginative and reminiscent of an actual sculpture exhibition.

Human Sculptures

Following *Sculpture Garden*, the couples are now asked to recreate the form and feeling of their sculpture with their bodies. It is not enough to copy the general shape, nor very satisfactory, since the human body is constructed differently than a chair. But if, for example, the sculpture is asymmetrical, with a feeling of stretching forth, that is what the players should try to express. After a few moment's practice, the couples take turns to demonstrate their results beside their opus. This exercise can give us a new insight into what it was in the "sculpture" that gave aesthetic pleasure.

Variation I

We can now try to create a large-scale work with all the members of the group cooperating to build a sculpture with all the chairs. Here, in addition to the need for the aesthetic cooperation and sensitivity needed to build some creation with a feeling of unity, several other skills are developed. For instance, players quickly encounter "engineering" problems to get their chairs to stack in the desired form without their becoming unstable and overbalancing. Incidentally, this is a valuable lesson in itself: an artist of any kind must always fit the imaginative concept to the practical means of execution — no concept is worth much if it is impossible to realize. I learned this very early on, watching my father, a professional sculptor who had trained as an engineer, building the armatures on which to model his sculptures. His compositions always had to fit the nature and physical characteristics of his chosen material. What suited bronze was totally wrong for a wood carving or terra-cotta.

Variation II

We can now move on to include other objects. The players make sculptures from random objects to be found in and around the workshop. For the inexperienced, "less" often means "more." Thus, using as few as two or three such objects usually creates a cleaner, more effective work than using too many. I recall one particularly witty "frog monster" made from a wastepaper basket, a couple of light bulbs and a felt hat. This happened to be representational, but totally abstract creations can also be satisfying. One work consisting of a broom resting on a larger broom was much admired.

Teachers have reported that this game can result in periods of intense concentration and furious activity. To keep the element of cooperation and a shared experience to the fore, I believe it advantageous to have children work in pairs.

If classroom conditions, or a dearth of suitable objects, make the creation of such a sculpture garden impractical, we can do the same thing in miniature, on a table top. Using the many small everyday objects readily available, including the contents of your "bag of tricks," if you have one (see above), we explore the possible combinations and create our little table top museum.

Exercises

• Go home and try to create sculptures from everyday objects found in the house and garden. If you can, take photographs of them to show to the group.

Variation III

As in *Variation I*, the whole group now cooperates to create a single, unified structure with the materials on hand. One can achieve very decent results with limited means, since this spurs the players on to find the most inventive ways of using available items. The structure can be quite abstract, or it can have a given theme. I have given my groups such images as a circus, the Fourth of July, and even a prison. The aim is not to create a literal, recognizable structure, but one that captures the feeling and rhythms of the image.

It is important that the natural leaders of the group not be allowed to dominate by directing the group effort. One way is to have each player add one specific item to the structure. This may cause frustration in those players who have an intensely individual approach and know exactly how they envisage the completed work. Don't worry! There is no attempt here to suppress individuality, which will have plenty of other opportunities for expression, but rather an attempt to demonstrate how a group can be creative in a special way, and can achieve results that the participants, working separately, could not manage.

I've tried this game with success with both children and adults. I gave one group of sixth graders a "fun fair" as their subject. Fifteen minutes of apparent chaos filled the room with a carousel, booths, a ghost train, a roller coaster and a fortuneteller. It wasn't exactly a sculpture, but a complete environment, and everybody had a rare time. On another occasion, a group of teachers decided to tackle a "war memorial." We all felt that the result did capture the feel, but wondered if it would get across to a stranger. Calling in a passing student we asked him to comment. "I'm sorry," he said, "but it just reminds me of a monument!" I'm not trying to imply that such exercises are always equally successful, or that "failures" are not frequent. It depends how you measure "failure." I truly believe that in these workshops, the only failure is the failure to participate. Every attempt is part of one's developing experience, and therefore is positive. Thus, one should always concentrate on those aspects of a group effort that are more successful, rather than indulging our tendency to criticize destructively.

Playground

This is a variation of *Sculpture Garden*, adapted for use with the very young. I've found it highly popular with classes of five- and six-year-olds. I start out with each child sitting on a chair and then ask the children to find different ways of sitting on the chair. One sits cross-legged, a second crouches, a third sits astride with arms resting on the back. Eventually, one child, maybe with prompting and maybe without, thinks of putting the chair on its side or upside down and sitting on it that way. Soon all the children are busily finding new ways of interacting with the chair.

I now ask them to work in pairs and make something from their two chairs. Cars, houses, planes, and spacecraft miraculously appear. Soon, by natural process, the children are working in groups of three or four. More chairs are pressed into service, plus any other material that can be found: a broom, a piece of wood, a coat. The room is filled with the happy noise of group activity. In one class I conducted at a youth art center, the children quickly developed the idea, and made great use of the many drawing boards on hand.

The teacher, in the meantime, is hard at it, visiting each group — riding in the car, or eating cake in the house, or arriving on the moon — while at the same time keeping four eyes open for children who have not managed to fit into a group, for quarrels over the possession of a chair, and so on.

For at risk children who may have difficulty in using their imagination to create play environments, this kind of activity is of particular importance. Chairs are at one and the same time solid, tactile, and reassuringly familiar, and an ideal medium in size and shape for imaginative constructions. It is for a similar reason that the building blocks developed by Caroline Pratt (described in *The Block Book*, edited by E. S. Hirsch) are big enough to form environments into which the children can enter.

Tall and Short

Up to this point we have been mainly dealing with transformation of external objects. Even in *Figure-It*, where we act out situations suggested by figure drawings, no particular emphasis has been placed on transforming *ourselves*, our physical being. A large part of theatre acting, of course, involves just that. The character an actor is called upon to portray often has distinct physical traits which reflect that character's personality. By discovering these external characteristics, an actor is helped to make contact with the inner life to be conveyed.

When we experience the world, our response to it is as much conditioned by our physical as by our mental states. I once knew a pretty, vivacious girl who fell from her bicycle when she was ten and was left with a scarred lip. She became self-conscious, lost her gaiety, developed a sarcastic wit, put on weight and, in short, developed a defensive shield that changed her personality entirely. This is an extreme case, but all of us are affected by our physical state and by our (frequently mistaken) self-image.

One way to re-evaluate ourselves, to increase our flexibility and adaptability, is to try to imagine ourselves in a different body. We can then see how our responses to the world around us seem to change. It can, however, be extremely difficult to envisage ourselves in another body, requiring a freedom of imagination which not everybody achieves with ease.

Here is an amusing game which can be enormously useful in overcoming this problem. Opera glasses or weak binoculars (children's toy binoculars are not bad) are required. The players look down at their own feet through the glasses, first using the magnifying end. Not only do the feet seem enormous but also very close to the eyes. As one tries to walk or jump, it is easy to imagine being short and heavy like some mythological dwarf. There is an extraordinary sense of being in another body.

Now the reducing end is tried and the effect is even greater. You are immensely tall and slender, your feet are far, far away, and it requires a good sense of balance to take even a few steps. In group sessions, no matter how many players have already tried this and their gasps of surprise noted, the next player to try will still be caught by the same surprise. It has a physical immediacy similar to the experience of trying to run with one's eyes shut described in *Solitaire*. Persevere for a minute or two before returning to "normal" and you will find that when you now look at your feet at their regular size, they seem a bit strange and unfamiliar.

If more that one pair of glasses is available, the players can work in pairs. Try dancing — it's quite an experience!

Children are entranced by the experience. They perform all sorts of antics, and afterward, when they are asked to become short or tall, without the aid of the glasses, they do so with a will. I have even been told that the game proved useful for children with body-image problems.

Art Gallery

The players enter the playing area one by one. It has become an art gallery. They must try to envision for themselves the shape of the room, the color of the walls, the sources of light and the sense of space. The walls are hung with paintings and the players must look at them, see them as clearly as possible and react to them as they would in a real gallery. The object of the game is not to act out these reactions, but purely to experience them. The paintings may be familiar or completely new to the individual player, who should be able to describe them if asked to do so. Up to this point the exercise is a form of a *Reality* game.

Now comes the first personal change. The players are asked to imagine themselves transformed — they are now three feet in height and 300 pounds in weight. This is their "given" condition — they must imagine that they have always been like that. Their task, however, remains the same — to look at the paintings and react to them. The game continues with the "given" condition changing from time to time. The players may become ten feet tall and be as light as balloons; they may be of normal size and weight, but have enormous Dumbo ears that trail on the ground but that are extraordinarily sensitive; they may have noses that, Pinocchio-like, stick out three feet from the face.

After the game a discussion can be held. What did it feel like? Was one particular condition especially vivid? How did the perception of the paintings change, if at all? One student mentioned how a painting that she had found attractive when normal, suddenly became rather menacing when she was tall and almost weightless. "I just couldn't look at it anymore," she said. Other players have remarked that it was strange to return to normal after the game— suddenly they were experiencing their bodies afresh.

You may ask why I suggest such grotesque given conditions. The answer is that as an initial exercise, such broad characteristics are likely to arouse a more immediate response in the players. Later on, one can suggest more "normal" transformations. For example, one interesting variation is to imagine yourself changed into the opposite sex. The players, themselves, can also be given a chance to suggest transformations.

The concept may prove difficult for some children. It can be hard to concentrate both on one's new physical being, and on the creation of a picture gallery. One teacher solved the problem by using real posters.

Exercises

• Choose another environment in which to play the above game.

• On your way home, or at any other convenient time, imagine yourself physically changed, as above. Afterward, write a diary entry about how you felt.

Music Moves

Children love to run and jump and dance and roll about. They freely give satisfying physical expression to their emotions, but all too quickly that freedom is lost. Society and our parents are much to blame; we mustn't dirty our clothes, we must be decorous and we must sit up straight. We begin to hide our feelings and suppress our impulse to express ourselves physically, doing so in socially acceptable ways only. Even when we go to the disco, our dancing is stereotyped and lifeless. We begin to feel imprisoned in our own bodies or alienated from them. This divorce of mind and body may be deadly for one's body is truly as much a part of the "self" as one's mind. As the psychologist R. D. Laing has said,

> Such a divorce of self from body deprives the (unembodied) self from direct participation in any aspect of the life of the world which is mediated exclusively through the body's perceptions, feelings and movements (expressions, gestures, words, actions, etc.). Instead of being the core of his true self, the body is felt as the core of a false self which a detached, disembodied, "inner true" self looks on at with tenderness, amusement, or hatred, as the case may be. (*The Divided Self*)

While the above description is extreme, most of us have experienced such feelings in some degree, at some point in our lives.

Music Moves is a series of exercises of great fundamental importance, in that it can help us to become aware of our physical inhibitions and to question them. It can then help us to think, imagine and respond with our total self. We seek to rediscover our childlike freedom of bodily expression.

Great sportsmen or women let the body respond directly to the demands of the moment. As a famous baseball coach once remarked, "Every time you think, you hurt the ball club." He did not mean that thinking is bad, but that it should mostly take place during training sessions, during which it becomes so integrated into the player's being that it becomes physically instinctive. And here is the poet W. B. Yeats trying to account for the fact that a certain stranger was vulgar.

> His arm and hand, let us say, moved in direct obedience

to the head, had not that instinctive motion that comes from a feeling of weight, of the shape of an object to be touched or grasped...The result was an impression of vulgarity, defiance of what is old and profound and simple.

Preliminary Exercise — Moving Pictures

The players listen to a piece of music and concentrate on allowing visual images to form in their minds. Such images may be fleeting and vague, or powerful, stable and detailed. Players should gradually find it easier to "fix" such images with practice, developing them in concrete terms of color, movement, landscape, figures or action.

Most people would agree that music can arouse these images. While one work is wild and somber, another is civilized and delicate, and a third is joyous and energetic. Players should become accustomed to performing the exercise to music of widely differing styles. I usually refrain from telling the name of the work in advance and select short pieces likely to be unfamiliar to the players, in order to avoid preconceived images. As a result an extraordinary range of ideas can be reported, sometimes in opposition to each other and even when the composer has intended something quite specific. Despite Richard Strauss's claim that he could depict the very color of a girl's hair, music remains a very subjective medium. When the composer Franz Liszt heard Felix Mendelssohn's "Scottish" symphony for the first time, he was mistakenly told it was the "Italian" and commented rapturously on the Italian atmosphere of the music.

Some players object to this use of music, claiming that for them it has purely aural associations, or that the exercise somehow exploits the purity of the music. I can only say that no attempt is being made to distort the way a person usually chooses to listen to music. Similarly, experimental productions of Shakespeare which may or may not work in their own terms, do not "destroy" the original work.

At risk children can also find it hard to associate a visual image with music. For example, when I asked one class what they saw when I played a solo guitar piece, they replied — with some logic — "a man playing a guitar." However, if vivid music is used and the right questions are asked, the children soon tell you whether the music is happy, sad, peaceful or violent. Then they tell you that they see red colors, or cowboys riding, or a king and queen. Also, cinema and television have familiarized most children with the sounds and purpose of background music.

The first essential is that the players be encouraged to express their responses in any way they can. When I asked the above-mentioned children to draw pictures of what they saw, most of them drew guitars, though some dancing figures also appeared. I then asked them to draw the *sounds* coming out of the guitar. This was not an easy concept for them, but after we talked about the sounds — were they sharp, smooth, long, short, all one color or mixed, they drew happily away. Some of the images they produced were remarkably vivid.

For a further discussion, see the section below called *Drawing to Music.*

Enter the Picture

The players spread out and when they have found a relaxed posture and are concentrating, the music begins. Each player concentrates on the visual image the music is generating and simply tries to "enter the picture" and move about inside it. Nothing should be planned and a freely flowing combination of stretching, turning, sliding, jumping, crouching and pantomimed actions should emerge.

Now this is easy to say, but for most people it is extremely hard to do, especially in the early stages. Even when a degree of group trust has been achieved, our bodily inhibitions are so great that the most tentative or banal movements seem to require an intense effort of will. Discomfort, frustration and even anger are frequently apparent. Many and varied are the excuses and rationalizations offered. "The music is unsuitable." "I've got boots on." "The music's so beautiful I just want to sit and listen." "How do you expect us to move? We don't know what to do!"

It is true that it is difficult to follow a bodily impulse if you are not sufficiently in tune with your body to discover what that impulse is. One lady told me with some defiance, "O.K. You told me to follow my impulse. It told me to sit down." Whatever defensive posture is being adopted, however, the essential lesson is being learned, the essential question is being asked. "Why do I feel so uncomfortable when asked to move freely? Why have I lost the freedom I enjoyed as a child?"

Once the basic problem has been experienced and discussed, I usually put on a modern pop number and encourage the group to move, even within the somewhat stereotyped framework of pop dancing. Some relief is generally felt that movement is still possible after all and the players usually end the exercise feeling more positive. It should nevertheless be noted that I do not refer to this exercise as *Group Dance*. While nothing is forbidden, one of the aims is to get away from preconceived patterns of movement associated with various kinds of music. I sometimes use a particular piece of jazz. Many players, recognizing the jazz form, start happy pop-dance patterns. They use the music to provide the beat but ignore its deeper emotional content. It happens to be the signature tune of "Johnny Staccato," a violent urban crime series shown on television some years ago. The music is by no means "happy"; it is harsh, violent and cruel. I know this seems to counter what I said about the subjective nature of listening to music, but the point is that most of the "happy" dancers agree that the piece is anything but happy. They then realize that their movements, rather than being true personal responses, arose from a preconceived notion of the kind of movement suitable for jazz. They hadn't really listened. If someone has a genuinely different reaction to the music than that intended by the composer, it is perfectly legitimate and acceptable.

Another example: when well-known ballet music is used one sees many gestures and movements imitative of classical ballet. I again suggest that a preconceived notion is interfering with a true personal response. I remember one student who had spent years in ballet classes and was incapable of anything else; no matter what kind of music was played, the same stereotyped gestures emerged. This was closely bound up with her desire to present a dainty, elegant, aesthetic image of herself to the world. It's a good example of what the psychologist Jung partly meant about "the consciousness" interfering with the natural psychic processes.

In *Surprise Yourself*, we allow our hands to reach out and "find" objects in space which may then transform themselves without planning. Here, when we move to the music, we try to let our whole self reach out and discover a flow of images, also without conscious planning. If a response is right and natural we need not worry about how we look — for it cannot be ugly! I have suggested that if you cannot find an impulse to follow you should concentrate on finding an image of a visual environment into which to enter. If this does not seem to work for you, do not sit down or stand around doing nothing. Try to find any kind of movement at all and *keep moving*. As most professional authors can tell you, if you wait for inspiration to strike, you won't get much done. An exercise like this requires intense work and effort to overcome the inhibitions of years. If you talk to people who have lost their sight or hearing, you will learn that the sharpening of the remaining senses does not happen effortlessly but requires constant practice.

Exercises

- If you feel shy or inhibited, try this exercise at home, on your own. Choose a piece of music you like, and move around freely.
- Bring a recording you think is particularly suitable to the workshop.

Group Moves

Up to now I have talked about *individual* responses to *personal* images. However, the players are not on their own but are part of a group. As we learn to move freely in the playing area we become aware of the movements of the others. Just as the music acts as a stimulus, so must the players accept and respond to the swaying, stabbing, jumping, plunging and pantomiming going on around them. We cannot command the other players to move in a particular way and must allow ourselves to be influenced by them, just as they must accept *our* contribution.

Elements of movement, imagery and rhythm will begin to flow from one to another and be repeated, echoed, developed and counterbalanced. As the players gain in confidence and experience, more overt cooperation appears. In twos and threes they form and reform in varying combinations, sometimes unifying at climactic moments. Onlookers have occasionally remarked that it was hard to believe that the group had neither rehearsed nor discussed the piece beforehand, nor had it been deliberately choreographed. Such levels of achievement, however, are quite rare, and if the result is a bit chaotic, no matter — it is usually a function of the limited time available to repeat the exercise.

Thus, while in the initial stages it's okay to concentrate on individual responses; the group element should be emphasized as soon as the players have become accustomed to "tuning in." Some players tend to let others take the lead, reflecting and working to their images rather than making an equal contribution. This may be the solution adopted by those who have difficulty overcoming their physical inhibitions, but may also be the result of a mental laziness — a rejection of the effort needed to discover one's own personal images. Sometimes students seem to expect the group leader to provide all the impetus and enthusiasm needed to make a workshop a success. While most teachers will do their utmost to build and maintain a good atmosphere, especially with children or at risk groups, in the end one reaps what one has sown. So don't give up if this is one activity which does not seem to bring instant satisfaction.

Given Images

Once the players have practiced finding their own images and movement, we can take the step of providing a central image from which they can work. Sometimes it is enough to name the musical work ("The Drowned Cathedral," by Debussy, or such jazz pieces as "The Train and the River" — Jimmy Guiffre, or "Swing That Hammer"). With Israeli groups I have used a highly evocative Jewish work, the "Nigun" from the "Baal Shem" suite by Ernest Bloch, giving them the following image: the daily life, celebrations and tragedies of the departed world of the Jews of the holocaust. This powerful image combined with the passionate music has given rise to some astonishingly intense group movements. Another effective combination used the opening passage of Stravinsky's "Rite of Spring," with the image of a primeval forest; as the sun rises there is a stirring and awakening of primitive life.

It can be useful to play a particular piece more than once. As long as they do not try to plan their movements in advance, the players are helped if they know the shape of the music, where the climaxes come and how and when it ends. It is always more aesthetically satisfying when the players are able to bring a sense of form to their work, with a beginning, development and end.

Animals

One teacher obtained excellent results from her special education class. She played music from "The Carnival of the Animals" by Saint-Saens and the children became the animals, moving freely about the room in time to the music and in many cases really captured the feel of the various animals.

There is a salutary difference between children and many of the adults with whom I have worked. Were I to ask them to become animals and prance about in joyous freedom their embarrassment would be crippling. They could sit quietly and describe beautiful or violent images, but only in verbal terms — they have become tentative and ashamed of their bodies. The Puritan ethic has still much to answer for.

Finger Theatre

As we all know, hands can be very expressive. We use them all the time to reinforce understanding, for emphasis, to convey emotion and in reaction to virtually every momentary contact with our world. Except when we deliberately plan them, our gestures tend to be unconscious reflections of our state of mind. In the following games and exercises we concentrate on our hands and allow them to develop a character of their own, trying to rediscover our own individual expressiveness through them.

Preliminary Exercise — Floppy Fingers

In this preliminary exercise, the players focus on their own hands. They hold them out in a relaxed manner and let them move freely. Waving up and down, exploring the space around them, caressing each other, our hands take on, as it were, a life of their own. The players now try to sense what "state of mind" the hands are in. Are they smiling or nervous or afraid? Does one hand act differently from the other? Do they react to each other, and if so, how?

Now the players try to imbue their hands with various emotions. How do they look if they are angry, depressed, excited or loving? What does a hand look and feel like when it is laughing? A crucial point arises here. *Every emotion is specific.* There is no reality to generalized laughter or fear: one laughs at something specific, is afraid of something specific and that something evokes a specific reaction. The fear of a wasp buzzing in your ear is quite different from the fear experienced if your car skids at high speed on an icy road. The laughter of two lovers plunging down a roller coaster is scarcely the same as the laughter greeting a dirty joke.

Two Hands in Search of an Author

The players now try to create a short scene using both hands. They can either think of an idea and then try various ways of carrying it out, or can allow their arms to move at random until a subject suggests itself. One student experimenting this way showed us a very charming scene of two horses galloping across a meadow, stopping to crop the grass and nuzzle each other and then galloping away. As long as it is lively and evocative a scene need not be particularly dramatic or have a highly developed plot. Whether it lasts for a few seconds or several minutes it should, however, have a beginning, middle, and end. I also find it useful to demonstrate to the group that it is better to hold the hands in natural positions when representing people, rather than using two fingers to act as legs walking about, which makes any emotional expression very difficult. After practicing on their own, the players show their scenes to the rest of the group.

Here is part of one teacher's report on the game:

The children are in a special class, aged from eight to eleven. From experience, I found it necessary to explain to the children that they did not have to guess exactly what was being represented — that if they saw two characters fighting they didn't have to guess if they were boxers or children. If they saw one animal pouncing on another they didn't need to know whether they were cat and mouse or tiger and antelope. This was necessary in order to encourage the children to show their ideas to each other.

The children thus thoroughly enjoyed performing their scenes and guessing what was being shown. Of course, it is possible to deepen the sensitivity and ability to distinguish between various acts, animals, etc. For instance, after practice, one child could show the difference between the way a horse trots and a man jogs. But the development of the imagination and enjoyment in performance seem to me to be the most important elements in the game.

What did the children show? A snake swallowing an egg. Two children playing jump rope (I developed the game, letting the children work in pairs). A sea anemone catching a little fish. A fisherman catching a fish. Ballet dancers. An obstacle race. Doing the high jump. A tiger pouncing on a deer. Two people arguing violently and then making up. A rifle poking out of a bunker and firing in all directions. A deputation arriving to meet the president.(!) A flower opening in the sun. Two cars colliding.

I think this report emphasizes just how inventive even at risk children can be when given the proper encouragement. Some of the ideas are extraordinary and in my adult groups I rarely see such a variety of pleasing topics.

Exercises

• Devise other ways of using the hands as "characters" in scenes.

• Try combining the hands of two players to create a "character."

Talking Fingers

We can now add sound effects and dialog to create something similar to a puppet theatre without the puppets. If one succeeds in imbuing one's hands with character, they seem to take on an independent life and as the scene progresses one can find oneself quite fascinated, wondering how it is going to develop. It is a similar experience to that felt by novelists who find that their characters have "taken charge."

The daughter of a friend of mine has cerebral palsy and her movements are stiff, jerky and uncoordinated. One day when I was visiting them, I asked her to show me a scene between a king and his servant. She was able to show us the proud, stiff, upright king and the humble, pliant and bowed servant. She enjoyed acting this out with her hands, spontaneously adding dialog, speaking both parts and altering her voice (also affected by her palsy) appropriately. Her father later told me that this visit sparked off a whole series of such scenes.

Exercises

• Try combining the hands of two players to create a more complex scene.

Change Change Change

This is a difficult exercise involving transformation, spontaneity, sensitivity, communication and cooperation. It is suitable for serious groups of various ages who have already tackled improvisations of other types. The teacher allocates numbers to the members of the group in order to establish the order of play. The first two players then enter the playing area and establish eye contact for a few moments. Neither has chosen a character beforehand, nor has any relationship between them been planned. As they look at each other they try to allow characters and a relationship to occur to them on impulse. As long as the players trust the moment and each other, the characters will emerge. This moment of surprise and release when one imagination leaps forth to mingle with another can be the most rewarding of all moments in creative play. When this level of trust is not so well established, what tends to happen is that one of the players initiates a relationship by action and words and the other player accepts the situation and plays along. While this is acceptable in early sessions, the teacher should try to encourage an equal sharing of responsibility for creation of the moment.

Once a relationship has been established, Player Three enters the playing area and Player One leaves, no matter what point the scene has reached. Players Two and Three now confront each other and a transformation takes place. Two entirely new characters emerge and a new relationship is discovered. Note that Player Two does not retain the same character. The exercise continues until the entrance of Player One brings the circle to a close.

Variation I

If the game is too difficult or confusing for children, a simpler version can be devised. The players are all allocated characters. The first two improvise whatever scene comes to them. Then Players Two and Three create a new scene, but Player Two stays in the same character. The scene may be a continuation of what went before, grow out of it, or be at a quite different time and place.

In one class the first two children were a rich man and a beggar meeting on the street. The beggar asked for charity which the rich man at first refused and then handed over some coins. The third child, playing a policewoman entered, the rich man left and the policewoman told the beggar to move along. When the beggar complained, he was threatened with arrest. The fourth player played a shopkeeper and rushed on as the beggar left, yelling that he had been robbed.

It is sometimes frustrating to have a promising scene broken off in the middle, so the teacher can exercise discretion and allow it to carry on a little longer. It is always more effective, however, to keep a scene short and leave the onlookers wanting more, than to drag it out.

Exercises

• Try to observe the world around you and discover other instances of the momentary transformation of objects into something else. Look for ways in which people adapt objects to uses for which they were not originally intended. Note these down and report back to the group.

UNIT 10:
CHARACTERS AND STORIES

Please tell me a story.
— Every child that ever was.

Introduction

While many of the games up to this point contained dramatic elements, role-playing, dialog, storytelling or character development, they were within the context of coordination, sensitivity, transformation, or reality games. Now we concentrate on the fun to be had playing roles, developing scenes and situations and telling stories.

Who's Who?

One of the players leaves the room. The others choose a well-known character, taken from history, literature, fairy tales, the Bible, or present-day life. The player returns and is helped by the group to discover who he or she is supposed to be. They adopt various roles other than the character and with him or her, act out scenes, confrontations, and episodes appropriate to the character in question. The player must participate and react freely, even without yet knowing who the character is, reacting in whatever way seems logical in light of the information so far gleaned. Once the player understands who the character is, he or she conveys this through the action, rather than calling out, "Oh, I know! I'm supposed to be so and so!" It is usually quite clear when the player is right, in which case the scene comes to an end, or wrong, in which case the scene continues.

For example, on one occasion the chosen character was Charlie Chaplin. One of the players started things off by "interviewing" him for a film magazine. When his replies were comically inappropriate the interviewer put this down to his "droll and idiosyncratic genius." A second player then tried chasing him around the room bellowing with hunger and yelling that he was a chicken — the famous scene from "The Gold Rush." This still didn't click with the subject, so a third idea was tried. A couple of players turned themselves into the automatic feeding machine from "Modern

Times" (their experience in *Machine* came in handy). Finally understanding, the subject started to twitch convulsively and shuffled around the room wielding a pair of imaginary wrenches.

With adults and teenagers, one quickly discovers that the main problem is not how to convey the needed information, but how to avoid giving the game away too easily. With younger children, the main problem is choosing a character whom everyone knows. Another problem is the difficulty some children have in choosing roles for themselves, or the best scenes from the character's life. One teacher thus found it necessary to allocate a role to each child before bringing the subject back. When the subject was Cinderella, for instance, she allocated the roles of the ugly sisters, the stepmother, the fairy godmother, the prince, and even the mice to pull the carriage. Here's how the scene went:

First Ugly Sister:	Clean the room! It's dirty!
Second Ugly Sister:	Get me something nice to eat. I'm hungry!
Subject:	*(Not yet knowing who she is)* I don't want to.
Mother:	Shut up and do what you're told. Just for that you can stay home while we go to the party. *(The three of them leave.)*
Good Fairy:	*(Appears.)* Poof! Do you want to go to the party, too?
Subject:	*(Beginning to understand)* Yes, but I don't look nice.
Good Fairy:	Don't worry, I got a super dress for you. Put it on.

From here on, although it was clear that the girl knew who she was playing, the teacher let the scene continue to give everybody a chance to take part. It should be noted that these children were familiar with the game. In the early stages, it may be necessary to do more prompting, take roles oneself and organize the scene as this teacher did. There can be a good deal of messy shouting and interruption in the beginning. Even adult groups can descend into chaos until they get the hang of it.

Exercises

- Make a list of characters suited to your group. Offer them to the group leader.

One Plus One

A player decides on a character and a place, enters the playing area and starts an appropriate activity, for instance, a man working in a garden. We call this the "starter." A second player, having identified the activity, also chooses a character and has the responsibility of establishing a relationship with Player One. Let's say she enters, apparently carrying some kind of basket. She says, "I thought we'd put the coleus in the corner next to the wall, darling. I'd like these cuttings over there, they need less sun." She has established herself as the gardener's wife; hopefully he picks this up, and the scene can continue in any direction. It should thus be noted that each player has a responsibility. Player One establishes the "Where," and Player Two establishes the relationship between the two characters.

Once it is clear to all who the characters are and what they are doing, the scene can come to an end or can continue to a natural conclusion as long as interest is maintained. There is often a tendency to look for a "plot," but unless it grows organically out of the situation and characters it can become forced, melodramatic, or jokey.

When concentration on character and place have become habitual, we can switch emphasis to the "What." That is to say, what do the characters want, and what are they doing? Let us suppose that in the gardening scene we give the two characters something which they each want — in theatrical terms, an "objective." She wants the nicest garden in the street, and is anxious because a society friend is coming to visit tomorrow, but the husband wants to stop to watch a ball game (or it could be the man who wants to impress someone, while his wife actually hates gardening). This introduces a natural source of dramatic conflict to the scene.

Exercises

• Make a list of possible starters suited to your group. Offer them to the group leader.

Keep It in Mind

An objective gives the actor in an improvisation a purpose, something to be achieved that leads a character to behave in a certain way. It is not always advantageous to predefine an objective, for this can unnecessarily limit the direction that a scene can take. However, it is often useful to give the character some circumstance, state of mind, or condition, that affects that character's attitude to what is happening in a particular scene. For instance, if — to return to the gardening scene in *One Plus One* — the wife has just been told by her boss that she is up for promotion, but only if she is prepared to relocate, and she doesn't know what to tell her husband, the entire thrust of the improvisation will be altered. Only the player acting the wife should know about it, since this removes from the player acting the husband the onus of acting *as if* he doesn't know. By selecting a variety of such circumstances for each of the characters, the same basic situation can develop in an infinite variety of ways.

You'd Never Guess

An amusing way of introducing tension and interest into basically run-of-the-mill situations, is to tell one or more of the players something about the *other* characters that they, themselves, are not told about. One situation that I have found can spark off inventive and spontaneous reactions from quite inexperienced players is the following:

Two new tenants have just moved into an apartment block. They are invited to have coffee in the apartment of two of the members of the house committee, who wish to welcome them and make them feel at home, inform them of the house rules, gardening and cleaning charges, and so on. I privately inform the hosts that when the new tenants arrive they are both perfectly bald, though otherwise normal. The guests are told that the inside of the hosts' apartment is filthy and smelly. Note that I don't tell the players playing the guests that they are bald, and don't tell the hosts that their apartment is filthy. All the players, therefore, act as if they are quite normal. While common politeness on both sides prevents direct comment, the situation is extreme enough to cause all sorts of uneasy exchanges. If the audience is in on the secret, much amusement ensues.

A discussion after the exercise usually reveals that while this situation is itself absurd, it is rooted in a basic aspect of society — we all have private opinions about the people around us that color our attitude toward them, even if we keep our thoughts to ourselves.

Keep It in Mind can be incorporated into almost all of the dramatic improvisation exercises.

Exercises

• Think of other situations suited to *You'd Never Guess*. Offer them to the teacher without telling the rest of the group.

The Dress-Up Box

An important part of make-believe consists of dressing up. Costumes add greatly to the fun, stimulating the imagination, adding color and liveliness to scenes and helping us to "become" the characters we are playing.

However, every parent knows how much time and effort can go into the creation of a complete costume for a party or school play. It is obviously impractical to attempt proper costuming every time we want to improvise a situation or story in a workshop.

With the players' help, the director or group leader should set about building up a collection of bits and pieces: discarded hats or caps, handbags, old fancy dress costumes, scarves, blouses, skirts, jackets, and bits of material, together with some specific props, toys, and pieces of wood, that can be adapted to the needs of the moment. Nothing elaborate or expensive is necessary, and the collection can be allowed to grow naturally. Additions will be greeted enthusiastically and their possibilities explored. Children can be helped to understand that a hat or jacket is often enough to give the "feel" of a character and that a walking stick can happily represent a scepter, horse, rifle, or doorway of a house.

Dress-Up Theatre

The simplest way to use the costume box in the creation of stories is to have each player go to the box and select one, or at a maximum, two items. When everybody is dressed, the players now decide who they are. In small groups they can now use these characters to create improvisations or to build stories that can then be acted out.

When I was in a group performing improvisations, our director had the habit of suddenly calling out, "You've thirty seconds to show me a silent movie!" or something of that sort. We'd rush to the dress-up box, find an item or two, and the first to be ready would enter the playing area and start a (hopefully) appropriate activity. The others would join in as the opportunity offered.

On one occasion she demanded "a Japanese movie." I found an old string bag that I shoved on my head as a hat, and a large round black velvet hat lacking a crown that reminded me of a shield. I thrust my arm through the hole in its center and, being the first, advanced to the front of the stage as a samurai warrior, bowed, and addressed the audience in "Japanese" gobbledygook. This gave three of the other players time to come on as another samurai, a geisha girl, and an old servant. They sat on the floor and the samurai imperiously demanded tea (also in gobbledygook). I retreated to the side and observed the ceremony. Another player took up her position at the other side and started to "narrate" the action in gobbledygook song. The geisha started a tea ceremony.

I now became jealous and confronted the second samurai. Snarling, growling, and uttering guttural threats, we challenged each other, drew our imaginary swords and attacked — just missing each other. This happened again, and then, on the third attempt, we allowed our swords to clash. As if pre-rehearsed, we both suddenly turned around simultaneously — I "killing" the old servant and he the geisha, who were cowering behind us. The narrator then brought the proceedings to a solemn close. I have rarely felt such a sense of empathy or sureness that my thoughts and those of the other players were so perfectly in tune. This was one of the very few improvisations that we were ever able to "set" and repeat, and it was always a hilarious success.

Tell Us a Story

Making up your own story, while it can be one of the most satisfying forms of group experience, can also be frustrating. Sometimes nothing seems to work — characters don't fit, and ideas either won't come or are trivial. At such times, a well-known story is just the thing to get energy flowing again. And of course, children love to hear well-loved, well-known stories over and over again. In this case, we're going to combine the best of both worlds; we're going to tell a well-known story and act it out at the same time.

The teacher should always involve children in the decision-making process — what story to choose and which of the children should play which roles. This done, the children choose suitable costume pieces and once they have become used to their characters, the story can begin. "Once upon a time..." The children act out the story as it is told, making their entrances and exits, pantomiming the actions, and making up the dialog. Whoever is acting as narrator, often but not necessarily the teacher, must make sure not to incorporate the words of the dialog into the narration, but to indicate what it is about. The narrator might say, "Mother warned Little Red Riding Hood of the dangers of the forest and told her what to do." This helps the child playing the mother to make up her lines. If a child fails to fill in the text you can encourage fuller participation by adding further ideas and not giving up. During a telling of *The Bremen Town Musicians* by the Brothers Grimm, the robbers sat around doing very little while I related how they ate and drank greedily. So I said, "The robbers were so greedy, they grabbed sausages and cake out of each of each other's hands and spilled the wine and yelled at each other." This did the trick and the robbers happily snarled and tussled and grabbed.

The Magic Material

Although it is useful to build up a dress-up box, overdependence on it can be restricting. Luckily, there is a magic material that can be transformed in a multitude of costumes or props — newspaper! You need an ample supply of old newspapers, scissors, adhesive tape, staplers, glue, and paper clips. Don't forget a broom, dustpan, and large garbage bags.

The players choose a simple story or situation to act out. They then set about creating all the costumes and props they need. It will quickly be discovered that virtually everything can be invented — hats, masks, beards and long flowing hair, baskets, flags, dresses, shawls. A narrow, tightly rolled tube of newspaper can make a surprisingly strong stick to support a banner or become a walking stick or sword, or can be bent into a circle to form the rim of a wheel or the handle of a basket. Start the tube by rolling the corner of a sheet diagonally around a pencil. A double page of newspaper will provide a good tube nearly a yard long and adding extra sheets can extend it as desired.

A story like *Little Red Riding Hood* contains any amount of props and costumes and teachers have reported exceptional enthusiasm as the children snipped, stuck, tried out, exchanged ideas and gleefully demonstrated their finished products. Although it is not essential, the work can be embellished by painting it in suitable colors. For this, gouache is the most effective.

A word of warning: This magic material produces strictly disposable costumes and props. Children should be helped to understand that their value lies in the fun of making them and in their immediate effect. If they are really charming, snap a few photos for a visual record.

Headlines

Throughout this book, I have emphasized the need to break away from stereotypes if true creativity is to be released. This is true of storytelling as well. Here is one method that uses the newspaper to stimulate the imagination. The group divides up into sub-groups of some half dozen players. Each player searches through a newspaper and cuts out *one* interesting word from a headline. We use headlines simply because they are printed in large letters and are therefore convenient to handle. The sub-groups now take their words and try to arrange them into a sentence or sequence which is like a headline (at the director's discretion, a limited number of connectives may be added), and which suggests a story or situation. An imaginative group effort is called forth to solve the puzzle. For example, here are the words which one particular group of players had to work on: HIGHEST - PRODUCING - EXPERIENCE - PRAC-TICE - ROMANTIC - CHINESE. After much laughter and earnest debate, the following headline was arrived at: [A] CHINESE PRAC-TICE[S] PRODUCING [THE] HIGHEST ROMANTIC EXPERI-ENCE. Further debate gave birth to the following story line: an emperor in ancient China decrees that his fun-loving son must devote his life to developing some branch of philosophy. The son circumvents the edict by choosing "love" as his particular area of research and summons the most beautiful women in the kingdom to aid him in his experiments.

Having formulated their headline and the story behind it, the players must now act it out.

In another of my workshops the following improbable head-line emerged: WIFE [OF] SWEDISH OFFICER HOLDS ANTI-POL-LUTION RALLY [IN] SOUTH AMERICA. The class then created the scene using newspaper to make all the costumes and props as in *The Magic Material*. The officer appeared in hat and medals, the wife carried a large antipollution banner, dancing girls in swirling skirts sambaed around and a good time was had by all.

For younger or at risk children, the game can be simplified by having them cut out words that are *names* for things, such as RAIN, SHOPPING, or PLUMBER. The teacher can then help them make up and act out a simple story involving these items.

Tall Tale

Another way to stimulate the creation of a story is to ask for suggestions of articles, animals and, maybe, ideas that must be linked together in a logical way. I remember one story which resulted from the choice of a HEDGEHOG, a NEWSPAPER and a SMALL BOY. The boy goes out for a walk in the park with his dog. They come across a ball of newspaper lying in the path at the bottom of a little rise. The ball seems to move and when the dog sniffs at it, it jumps back yelping in pain, and then barks angrily. The boy investigates, and carefully unwraps a hedgehog from the newspaper. A mystery! Luckily the hedgehog and dog speak animal language and the hedgehog explains that it was out foraging up the hill when it was frightened by a large dog. It rolled into a ball to protect itself and rolled down the hill onto the newspaper, getting all tangled up. They can't explain this to the puzzled boy, so they decide to re-enact the scene. The boy is delighted to have the mystery solved and then they all go home for tea.

Marionettes

Here is yet another way of stimulating original and amusing scenes. Two players choose, or have chosen for them, characters and a situation. Two other players are appointed as their "operators." The operators place their marionettes in physical postures, rather like in *Living Pictures*. The marionettes must now commence the scene, finding and incorporating a logical justification for these initial postures. As the action progresses, the operators *occasionally* intervene to alter the postures, again in any random way they see fit. They should usually do so when the action and invention seem to be flagging and should refrain from doing so if the scene is working well. One operator might make the character kneel while the other causes the second character to extend both arms up in the air. Once more, it is the actors' task to continue the scene in a logical way. The operators must not indulge in directorial placement — that is, they should not choose postures that clearly indicate a particular course of action, because they want the scene to go in a particular direction.

Beginning to End

Another way to force the players to seek fresh solutions to the development of situations is to have two players leave the room and choose their characters and a situation. In the meantime, the rest of the group chooses two random sentences that are written on the blackboard. One of the sentences is chosen as the opening sentence of the scene, while the other must bring it to a close. I say random sentences, because there is a tendency, once a first sentence has been chosen, to choose a second sentence that is logically implied by the first. I often wait till both sentences have been suggested and then choose the second one as the opener. The returning players often groan and complain when they see that their nicely planned scene has run into a major obstacle. Once they are a little more experienced, they refrain from that type of planning and concentrate on who the characters are, their preoccupations, and where they are. The opening sentence then comes as a challenge but also as a trigger, releasing creativity. "Hey, that's great," one of them will cry, "I know just what to do."

On one occasion, the two sentences were "I believe these belong to you," and "I told you not to forget the eggs!" Of course, I reversed them. In the meantime, the two players had chosen to be rival politicians appearing on television. Player A solved the first problem by turning to an imaginary third person off-stage, and whispering angrily, "I *told* you not to forget the eggs!" and then turning around, startled and embarrassed to find that the camera has been turned on. Toward the end of a lively exchange of political invective, a player not in the scene pretended to throw eggs at the second politician from the audience. Picking bits of egg off his face, he turned coldly to his rival and said, "I believe these belong to you." Thunderous applause!

This demonstrates another important lesson: All members of the group, including those not participating in a scene, should always be on their toes and involved in the action. If assistance is needed, an extra character, sound effects, or whatever, the other players should be ready to help out.

Trapped

This well-known theatre game can be highly dramatic but it can also develop in a comic way. Working in groups or pairs, the players act out a situation in which they are faced with some physical trap. An obvious example is "stuck in an elevator." Other scenes used in my workshops have included an encounter with a giant spider's web, quicksand, a fall of rock in a mine, lost in the desert, and trapped on a mountain threatened by an avalanche. This exercise involves quite a bit of *Use Your Whole Body* since all these situations are rich in sensory evocation and provide opportunities for bodily movement and struggle.

The scene should grow out of the physical problem and the reactions of the characters to it. In the beginning, players tend to create a scenario for themselves in which they finally escape the danger. As they become more sophisticated they allow the situation to lead them to destruction — the quicksand swallows them at last. This, too, should be seen as a phase. The player who truly allows the situation to develop without planning will never know if escape will come or not. That is, the player — *as player* — should not plan, although the character being played may very well do so. Whether the character's plans are successful or not will depend on the way the scene develops.

Exercises

• Think up as many situations for a *Trapped* scene as you can. Think how it can be combined with other games (such as *Beginning to End*).

The Great All-Purpose Do-It-Yourself Dialog

In the introduction to *Gobbledygook*, I suggested that our dependence on language goes hand in hand with our loss of contact with the very words coming out of our mouths. We rely on our words to convey our thoughts but find that those who hear us understand something quite different. The same words can have a multitude of meanings.

Here is a great game that shows just how many ways one dialog can be interpreted. Comic, dramatic, pathetic or absurd scenes can emerge. Working in pairs the players try to interpret the following dialog, choosing characters, place and situation, and discovering what is actually happening behind the exchange which is quite like a dialog in a play by Harold Pinter.

A: Well
B: So I'm here
A: I see
B: Yes
A: Well
B: That is all you can say
A: What do you want me to say
B: Nothing

127

A: Nothing

B: You don't trust me

A: That's not it

B: What is it

A: It doesn't matter

B: Stop that

A: What

B: That

A: I can't

B: Try

A: Better

B: It's hopeless

A: What is the matter

B: Don't know

A: Don't know

B: No

A: Tell me

B: Can't

A: Then go

B: I'll go

You will notice that I have included no punctuation marks. Many of the lines can be interpreted either as a question or not, can be addressed directly to the second party or can be muttered to one-self, to the audience, or an imaginary third party. Neither are pauses indicated, but can be meaningfully inserted in many places.

Probably the most obvious interpretation shows the final breakup of a relationship between a man and a woman. However, once the more obvious, or at least the more accessible, ideas have been tried out and have shown the way, more and more original ideas and situations can be discovered, some powerful and full of truthful emotion, and others delightfully absurd. One secret is to take nothing for granted, nor to assume the meaning of any word. The other is to look constantly for physical actions that give point and significance to the dialog.

For instance, in one highly inventive scene, a psychotic in a mental hospital (A) looking indifferently at an insecure young doctor (B) suddenly swung away and drew a happy smiling face on the wall (blackboard) with the word "Well" written beside it. Then with a savage gesture he scribbled all over it. This provided an excellent starting point for a quite original scene.

Another original idea had Adam awaken from a deep sleep, not notice Eve lying beside him, stretch his hands up to God and say, "Well?" Eve answered, "So I'm here." Unfortunately the silent serpent was present, smiling, seductive and fatally attractive to Eve, who at the end went to him and accepted the apple.

Unfaithful husband and jealous wife, two teenagers tickling each other, a mother and her rebellious daughter, a burglar and timid sidekick, a housewife and plumber who has come to fix a broken garbage disposal unit, two spies — the ideas come tumbling out.

Another scene — devised by two thirteen-year-olds — had a brash young journalist come panting into the office with his copy. The unimpressed older editor takes it up and starts to make corrections. When the youngster is offended and says, "You don't trust me," he is too busy scoring out and muttering, "That's not it," to hear him.

The first time a situation is tried out, it will lack many finer points of interpretation and enriching ideas. These can emerge with a little rehearsal and this is one game that requires the learning of the text by heart. Holding the script in the hand and looking at it all the time is terribly restricting. It prevents the discovery of all sorts of beautiful solutions to problems arising from the need to fit the text exactly into the situation. Under no circumstance should illogical actions or unexplained statements be allowed to remain, nor should lines be omitted because they don't seem to fit. The text should be regarded as sacred. If the players concentrate on the physical action, and allow the emotion to grow out of that, results will be original and creative.

Another fascinating twist is to take two characters who have already been worked out in a particular scene and switch their lines.

It is by looking for the unexpected and by tackling the apparently outrageous that truly original ideas can spring out of what seems to be the constricting framework of a piece of uninspiring dialog. But it is a framework that liberates the imagination by concentrating it, as a magnifying glass concentrates the rays of the sun and generates fire.

Exercises

• Think of several other ways of starting an original story line that can be either acted out or narrated.

• Try combining storytelling with other games and exercises taken from different sections of this book.

UNIT 11:
DRAWING TO MUSIC

Every child is an artist. The problem is how to remain an artist when one grows up.

Pablo Picasso

Without music life would be a mistake.

Friedrich Nietzsche

Introduction

When we are taught to draw as children, our creative freedom often regresses as our technical ability improves. Working with a group of at risk children I asked them to draw large masks based on the idea of "opposites," ugly and beautiful, white and black, happy and sad and so on. The class pointed to one boy admiringly, as the "best drawer" in the class. While some of the others energetically produced images of great freedom and power, he painstakingly drew a nicely colored, well-proportioned Native American in a feather headdress. It was utterly stereotyped and dull. Nor had it anything to do with my requested subject. The boy had already learned how to gain the approval of the adult world and had set out to win my approval by repeating a drawing with which he had already had success. He was wholly confused when I asked for freer, more spontaneous work. There is no doubt that this request was the antithesis of most of the concepts of learning, success, or creativity that he had been taught.

To encourage spontaneity and to physically relax their drawing arms, I use a well-known technique. I play music and ask the group to draw or paint according to the rhythms of the music and the things they see in their imagination as they listen. This may be hard for them to grasp, but a short period of discussion is usually enough to set them working. We listen to the music and talk about what they have imagined. I then play the piece again while they work.

Some Examples

The accompanying illustrations are a small sample of one session I held a couple of years ago with a group of sixth and seventh graders. I used two pieces of music on this occasion: the first, a jolly, bouncing version of "Second-Hand Rose" played on a pub piano, and the second, a traditional jazz version of "Swing That Hammer" (based on an old slave work song and containing an exciting solo for drums).

The session resulted in about twenty drawings, done with colored wax crayons on large sheets of white paper. Unfortunately, some of them cannot be reproduced effectively in black and white, while others are unavailable because the children insisted on taking them home to show their folks. The ones reproduced on pages 134-138, however, are quite a representative selection.

Illustrations 23 and 24 are both by a very charming, undersized, overactive boy, always smiling, always ready with a wisecrack and usually in some kind of hot water. Here his energy is channeled superbly into two free-flowing, rhythmic drawings. Number 24, sketched swiftly in one color, is a particularly effective image of a drummer in full flight. Note how full of movement the hands are and how much genuine enjoyment is evident in the set of the head and its expression.

Illustrations 25 and 26 are by another boy — physically the biggest in the class, sturdy, competent, quite a good electrician (his father's trade) but a slow learner. He, too, has chosen a single color and has produced two vigorous images: the savage is full of physical power, and the dancer — look at her hair — shows lots of movement. The restricted feet are just due to the fact that he ran out of room at the bottom of the sheet of paper. When I praised him, he decided to do a "proper" picture for me, working much more carefully in several colors. Despite choosing an "important and interesting subject," a semidemented character, known as "The Runner," who used to run around the boy's neighborhood, the result was an inferior, static picture. Significantly, the background buildings, to which he had paid less attention, were much more successful than the wooden figure on which he'd lavished most of his effort. This was the drawing he chose to take back to show his teacher and parents and which I cannot therefore reproduce.

Illustration number 27 is the result of another child's direct hand response to the rhythms of the music — a large wedge-shaped scribble, fanning out from the bottom right-hand corner and then elaborated. Note the two enigmatic fish or bird shapes flanking the main figure.

Illustration 28 was drawn by a usually quiet girl, suspicious of the world, often frowning with worry, easily frustrated, but capable of sudden flashes of enthusiasm and warmth. She kept asking for

132

the jazz piece, "Swing That Hammer," that I had played the previous week. When I put it on, she set furiously to work and then approached me with her worried smile to show me this jungle scene. There are lots of nice touches, but note the central tree in particular. Composed of sharp spikes, superimposed on handsomely curved and flowing lines, it has great vitality and combines the characteristics of the two trees on either side.

Diagnostic Aids

The act of drawing has its own logic and justification but, in addition, the pictures can frequently indicate psychological difficulties and can provide the alert teacher with diagnostic material. Although this is not the place for a detailed discussion of art therapy (nor do I pretend to have adequate training in that field), I have included the last two pictures to suggest what can be learned about a child's state of mind.

Illustration 29 shows commendable energy but it has been pointed out that the lines are all abrupt, broken, twisted and violent. The central figure is cut off from the ground and cannot reach the door on the far right which is hidden behind coils of heavy black lines, possibly smoke. A second rudimentary figure — identifiable by the lines representing fingers or toes clearly seen in the first figure — is broken up into chaotic fragments which echo the rest of the background. The child in question was certainly of below average ability and was full of frustration; he seemed to see the world as a frightening, confusing place, operating according to rules that he could not comprehend. However, without such a drawing to act as a clue, a teacher might well overlook the child's problem, since neither his general demeanor nor his behavior was particularly aberrant.

The girl who drew illustration number 30, though rather pretty (I mention this to indicate that her looks were no bar to her ability to socialize), was pale and apathetic. She would constantly declare that she "can't draw," but with encouragement, she produced angry, scary images. In this case, she seemed to ignore the music altogether, but her friend beside her drew a household scene in response to the pub piano (which she said reminded her of her mother doing housework), and we can see that she has also drawn a household scene. The sense of isolation is strong, with the two figures, framed in the curtained windows and separated from each other and the world by the furious black lines of the massive, overpowering walls. The female dominates, staring at us defiantly, hands on hips. The armless male looks at her forlornly. I asked her regular teacher if these could be her father and mother. "Yes," he said, "quite likely." The father was usually unemployed, the mother domineering, and the home situation very bad. He had visited the home and there seemed little possibility to alleviate the situation.

The girl returned to this subject a number of times. She seemed cynical about the praise she received for her work, but was less reluctant and was sufficiently interested in her drawings to lavish all her time in art class on them. Perhaps the two most important facts to emerge are these: we, her teachers, became more aware of her problems and she found a way of expressing her feelings. It was a start.

Illustration 23 — Face

Illustration 24 — Drummer

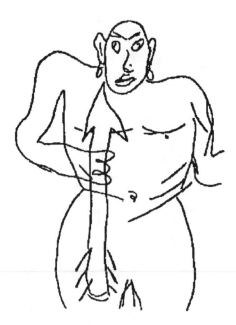

Illustration 25 — Savage

Illustration 26 — Dancer

Illustration 27 — Figure With Fish

Illustration 28 — Jungle Scene

Illustration 29 — Figures and Burning House

Illustration 30 — House With Parents

CREATIVE QUOTATIONS

The wisdom of the wise and the experience of the
ages are perpetuated by quotations.

Benjamin Disraeli

Introduction

Below are a number of aphorisms or sayings, all dealing in one way or another with the creative process. Read them and then try the following exercises.

Exercises

- Very often, when these sayings are read aloud, people will laugh and nod their heads. What is it about the humorous quotations that makes them funny? What are the truths underlying the general statements?

- Can you think of specific examples, taken from your own experience, from history, books, movies, etc., that illustrate the point made by any of the sayings?

- Group the quotations under different headings according to similarities between them. Can you remember other sayings that more or less make the same point? Can you remember sayings that seem to say the opposite? If so, compare the sayings and try to see what point each is making and whether both may contain aspects of the truth.

- Try to formulate your own aphorisms on creativity or any other subject. I tried this exercise myself, and managed to come up with a number of statements, which I list at the end of this unit. I doubt if they are particularly original, but I felt satisfied, because they came out of my own thinking.

  Nothing will be attempted if all possible objections must first be met.
  Well begun is half done.

Anonymous

139

I'm not young enough to know everything.

J. M. Barrie

Do not seek to follow in the footsteps of the men of old; seek what they sought.

Basho

A hunch is creativity trying to tell you something.

Frank Capra

No matter how old you get, if you can keep the desire to be creative, you're keeping the man-child alive.

John Cassavetes

One sees great things from the valley, only small things from the peak.

G. K. Chesterton

Teachers open the door, but you must enter by yourself.

Chinese Proverb

Music is the art of thinking with sounds.

Jules Combarie

No one travels so far as he who knows not where he is going.

Oliver Cromwell

The whole difference between construction and creation is exactly this: that a thing constructed can only be loved after it is constructed; but a thing created is loved before it exists.

Charles Dickens

Write as if you are dying.

Annie Dillard

Genius is one percent inspiration, and ninety-nine percent perspiration.

Thomas Edison

Everything should be made as simple as possible, but no simpler.

Albert Einstein

The creation of a thousand forests is in one acorn.

Ralph Waldo Emerson

In the creative state a man is taken out of himself. He lets down as it were a bucket into his subconscious, and draws up something which is normally beyond his reach. He mixes this thing with his normal experiences and out of the mixture he makes a work of art.

E. M. Forster

What you can do, or dream you can, begin it; boldness has genius, power and magic in it.

Goethe

To live is to have problems and to solve problems is to grow intellectually.

J. P. Guilford

It is good to have an end to journey toward; but it is the journey that matters, in the end.

Ursula K. Le Guin

If you can see in any given situation only what everybody else can see, you can be said to be so much the representative of your culture that you are a victim of it.

S. I. Hayakawa

One cannot step twice into the same river.

Heraclitus

Genius, in truth, means little more than the faculty of perceiving in an unhabitual way.

William James

Curiosity is one of the most permanent and certain characteristics of a vigorous mind.

Samuel Johnson

A person needs a little madness, or else they never dare cut the rope and be free.

Nikos Kazantzakis

The map is not the territory.

Alfred Korzbyski

An essential aspect of creativity is not being afraid to fail.

Dr. Edwin Land

In creating, the only hard thing's to begin; A grass-blade's no easier to make than an oak.

James Russell Lowell

It seems that the creative faculty and the critical faculty cannot exist together in their highest perfection.

Thomas Macaulay

Imagination grows by exercise, and contrary to common belief, is more powerful in the mature than in the young.

W. Somerset Maugham

I used to think anyone doing anything weird was weird. Now I know that it is the people that call others weird that are weird.

Paul McCartney

For every human problem there is a neat, plain solution — and it is always wrong.

H. L. Mencken

The only joy in the world is to begin.

Cesare Pavese

Computers are useless. They can only give you answers.

I do not seek. I find. (Je ne cherche pas; je trouve).

Pablo Picasso

Go — not knowing where. Bring — not knowing what. The path is long, the way, unknown.

Russian Fairy Tale

Necessity is the mother of invention, it's true — but its father is creativity, and knowledge is the midwife.

Jonathan Schattke

The chief cause of problems is solutions.

Eric Sevareid

There are no foolish questions and no man becomes a fool until he has stopped asking questions.

Charles Steinmetz

To travel hopefully is better than to arrive.

Robert Louis Stevenson

Every exit is an entry somewhere else.

Tom Stoppard

I have learned throughout my life as a composer chiefly through my mistakes and pursuits of false assumptions, not by my exposure to founts of wisdom and knowledge.

Igor Stravinsky

In the beginner's mind there are many possibilities, but in the expert's mind there are few.

Shunryu Suzuki

To do two things at once is to do neither.

The eyes are not responsible when the mind does the seeing.

Publilius Syrus

Our life is frittered away by detail…Simplify, simplify.

Henry Thoreau

Change is not merely necessary to life — it is life!

Alvin Toffler

The art of creation is older than the art of killing.

Andrei Voznesensky

I am a writer who came from a sheltered life. A sheltered life can be daring as well. For all serious daring starts from within.

Eudora Welty

We think in generalities, but we live in detail.

The "silly question" is the first intimation of some totally new development.

Every really new idea looks crazy at first.

Alfred North Whitehead

Be master of mind rather than mastered by mind.

Zen saying

Here, now, are my own attempts at aphorisms:

To be always right is a disaster.

Living is not measured in years.

To be wise is to be simple.

To the wise, work is play.

The clever know enough — the wise seek more.

There are no opposites, only continua.

Accepting advice is hard — especially your own.

The most deafening sound in the world is your own voice.

True freedom needs boundaries.

Not trying is the only true failure.

The real drama is backstage.

For any children, for any people, that want to do anything in life — if you visualize it and see it clear enough in living color, it's going to happen. I really believe it. As long as you're willing to work hard enough, it's going to happen.

Michael Flately, creator of *Riverdance*

SAMPLE WORKSHOPS

Introduction

Here are a number of sample workshop formats set up with various age groups in mind. I again emphasize that these are only guidelines. Before I conduct a workshop, I always note down a few suitable games and exercises to be used. However, I hardly ever stick rigidly to the plan. One exercise runs much longer than expected, another seems to lead naturally on to something else not planned, a participant makes a suggestion that is worth following up, or a particular game doesn't seem to click with the group, and something else is introduced instead.

In addition, the age groups are quite problematic. A particular group of youngsters may well enjoy a game thought of as suitable mainly for older children. It is here that the sensitivity and experience of the instructor comes into play. So, my suggestions here are to be seen only as rough guidelines.

General Formats

The very first workshop with a new group should start with an orientation session, and include a *Trust* exercise, *Developing the Senses*, a *Reality* game and, from *Transformation, Discovery and Spontaneity*, "It's a Bird, It's a Plane, It's Superdraw."

Later workshops all start with warm-ups, include some sense development, and a *Reality* game. They continue with games selected from other sections, such as *Coordination and Interaction, Sensitivity and Communication, Transformation, Discovery and Spontaneity*, or *Characters and Stories*.

a. *Warm-up exercise(s):* These should start with individual physical stretching, breathing and relaxation exercises, which the players perform after they arrive. There follows a brief session of group warm-ups conducted by the director.

b. *Orientation game:* Only performed in the first one or two workshops of a series.

c. *Trust exercise:* More time is spent on this exercise at the beginning of a course than later on, although they can be included once in a while thereafter.

d. *Developing the Senses:* Greater emphasis is placed on these games early on, but if the director feels that more advanced games and exercises are not achieving their full potential, he or she may go back to them.

e. *Coordination and Interaction:* The same comments apply to these games as to *Developing the Senses.* More advanced games mostly depend on coordination and interaction, so specific exercises need only be returned to if something is missing in their performance.

f. *Reality:* It is useful to come back to these games from time to time, to ensure that players constantly rediscover their contact with reality, but they need not be included in every workshop.

g. *Sensitivity and Communication:* Again, we return to these games and look for further developments of them, from time to time. It is useful to play the same game again, after players have developed some of their skills, in order to feel the progress that has been made, and see how much further the game can be taken.

h. *Transformation, Discovery and Spontaneity:* Some of these activities will find their greatest use relatively early in a series of workshops, but ones such as *Music Moves, Finger Theatre,* and *Change Change Change,* can be returned to again and again.

i. *Drawing to Music:* Use of this activity depends very much on the age and composition of the group. It can well be included in a course of workshops as a major activity in one or two sessions.

j. *Characters and Stories:* Clearly, these games, involving as they do, elements from all the other types of exercise, are the culminating test of the players' abilities. Introduced at a simple level as soon as possible, they have literally endless possibilities.

Sample Workshops

1. *1st to 3rd graders*	2. *4th to 6th graders*
Tag	Tag - Slow Motion Tag
Yum-Yum	Catch Me Falling
Unfolding Hands	Leading the Blind
King of the Circle	Follow Me
Light and Heavy	Unfolding Hands
Who's Who? or	Light and Heavy
Who Am I?	Who's Who?

3. *6th to 8th graders*

Tag – Slow Motion Tag
Kitty in the Corner
Listen to the Birdie
It's Stuck or Something
Rhythm Kings
One Plus One

4. *9th grade and up*

Tag – Slow Motion Tag
Leading the Blind
Blind Running
Space Walk
Space Adventure
Mirror
What's Going On?
One Plus One

Performance Workshops

At the end of a successful course, it is often a very good idea to hold an open workshop to which family and friends can be invited. Sample games from each category can be demonstrated, and suggestions from the audience accepted. Here, however, the skill and experience of the director are most important, to ensure that the group is ready, and to ensure that nervousness and self-consciousness do not ruin the session.

Selected Bibliography

Brook, Peter. *The Empty Space*. London: Avon, 1972.

Cassady, Marsh. *Acting Games*. Colorado Springs, CO: Meriwether Publishing Ltd., 1993.

Chiefetz, Dan. *Theater in My Head*. Boston: Little Brown and Co., 1971.

Creber, J. W. Patrick. *Lost for Words: Language and Educational Failure*. Harmondsworth: Penguin, 1974.

de Mille, Richard. *Put Your Mother on the Ceiling*. New York: The Viking Press, 1973.

Edwards, Betty. *Drawing on the Right Side of the Brain*. Los Angeles: J. P. Tarcher, 1979.

Hirsch, Elizaberth S. (ed.) *The Block Book*. Washington, D.C.: National Association for the Education of Young Children, 1974.

James, Muriel and Dorothy Jongeward. *Born to Win: Transitional Analysis*. Reading, MA: Addison-Wesley Publishing Company, 1971.

Koestler, Arthur. *The Act of Creation*. London: Hutchinson, 1964.

Marzollo, Jean and Janice Lloyd. *Learning Through Play*. Harmondsworth: Penguin, 1977.

Perls, Frederick, Ralf F. Hefferline, and Paul Goodman. *Gestalt Therapy*. New York: Delta, 1951.

Smilansky, Sara. *The Effects of Sociodramatic Play on Disadvantaged Preschool Children*. New York: John Wiley & Sons, 1968.

Spolin, Viola. *Improvisation for the Theater*. Evanston, IL: Northwestern University Press, 1963.

Novelly, Maria C. *Theatre Games for Young Performers*. Colorado Springs, CO: Meriwether Publishing Ltd., 1985.

ABOUT THE AUTHOR

Amiel Schotz has been actively involved in theatre and the arts since an early age. He was born and educated in Scotland, where his father was Sculptor to the Queen of England. He became an actor and theatre director at Glasgow University and later took his Master of Fine Arts in acting and directing at Brandeis University.

He emigrated to Israel in 1965 and has continued to direct and to act on both professional and amateur stages and on the screen. He took part in the first public performances of *Theater Games* in Israel. His poetry and other writings have appeared in various publications and newspapers. He is also an accomplished translator and editor.

For more than twenty years he has given courses and workshops in creativity and theatre games to groups ranging from preschoolers to old-age pensioners, from at risk children to professional teachers and actors. This book distills and concentrates his years of practical experience. Reading it comes as close to participating in his workshops as is possible without actually being there.

ORDER FORM

Meriwether Publishing Ltd.
P.O. Box 7710
Colorado Springs, CO 80933
Telephone: (719) 594-4422

Please send me the following books:

_____ **Theatre Games and Beyond #TT-B217**   **$15.95**
by Amiel Schotz
A creative approach for performers

_____ **Acting Games — Improvisations and**   **$14.95**
Exercises #TT-B168
by Marsh Cassady
A textbook of theatre games and improvisations

_____ **Theatre Games for Young Performers #TT-B188** **$14.95**
by Maria C. Novelly
Improvisations and exercises for developing acting skills

_____ **Everything About Theatre! #TT-B200**   **$16.95**
by Robert L. Lee
The guidebook of theatre fundamentals

_____ **Improve With Improv! #TT-B160**   **$12.95**
by Brie Jones
A guide to improvisation and character development

_____ **Improvisations in Creative Drama #TT-B138**   **$12.95**
by Betty Keller
A collection of improvisational exercises and sketches for acting students

_____ **Truth in Comedy #TT-B164**   **$14.95**
by Charna Halpern, Del Close and Kim "Howard" Johnson
The manual of improvisation

**These and other fine Meriwether Publishing books are available at
your local bookstore or direct from the publisher. Use the handy
order form on this page.**

Name: _____

Organization name: _____

Address: _____

City: _____ State: _____

Zip: _____ Phone: _____

❑ **Check Enclosed**
❑ **Visa or MasterCard #** _____

Signature: _____ Expiration
Date: _____
(required for Visa/MasterCard orders)

COLORADO RESIDENTS: Please add 3% sales tax.
SHIPPING: Include $2.75 for the first book and 50¢ for each additional book ordered.

❑ *Please send me a copy of your complete catalog of books and plays.*